GOLDENBALLS

Richard Ingrams

HARRIMAN HOUSE PUBLISHING

First published in Great Britain 1979 by
Private Eye Productions Ltd in association with
Andre Deutsch

First published in paperback by
Coronet (Hodder & Stoughton) 1980

This edition published 1993 by Harriman House,
9 Irene Road, Parsons Green, London SW6 4AL

British Library Cataloguing-in-Publication Data
A catalogue record for this book
is available from the British Library.

Printed and bound in Great Britain by
Bath Press, Bath.

ISBN 1 897597 03 7

'Few attacks either of ridicule
or invective make much noise
but by the the help of those
that they provoke.'

Dr Johnson

Contents

No Laughter in Court   1

The Clermont Set   8

The Eye Investigates   14

Here Comes the Judge   22

From Marzipan to Ermine   32

The Attempt to Settle   43

Volte-Face   54

The Perils of Peerage   68

The Injunction Hearing   77

A Matter of Contempt   92

A Setback   102

Biggles to the Rescue   110

Who Done it?   120

No Laughter in Court

For many people who do not read it, *Private Eye* is just the magazine that is always being sued. This is because the only time the public ever hears of it is when the newspapers report that a libel writ has been issued or an out-of-court settlement reached. The impression is therefore widespread that *Private Eye* is constantly being bombarded with writs and that at any moment it might go out of business as a result.

Yet to me the surprising thing is how seldom *Private Eye* is sued, considering the material it prints. At any time there are about ten or so libel actions pending against *Private Eye*, as opposed to about a hundred against Times Newspapers Ltd. Even so, the amount of libel actions per annum has probably increased since the early years of the *Eye*.

Since it began publication in 1961 the character of the magazine has gradually changed. When we started, it was a purely humorous or satirical paper consisting of jokes and parodies. But after Claud Cockburn acted as guest editor for an issue in 1963, we introduced a page of exposé journalism at the back of the magazine and the following year a gossip column at the front. Over the years both these features expanded, thanks mainly to Paul Foot who joined *Private* Eye in 1967 and subsequently produced a number of investigative scoops, notably the first national exposure of the Poulson affair. When Foot left in 1972, his place was taken by a number of writers working on a rather more freelance basis. These include Martin Tomkinson, Michael Gillard, a financial journalist formerly with *The Daily Express*, Patrick Marnham, who has contributed regularly since leaving Oxford in 1966, and Richard West. More recently they were joined by Nigel Dempster, the notorious gossip columnist of the *Daily Mail*.

Partly because it is a fortnightly magazine, *Private Eye* is produced in a rather haphazard way. It has no full-time staff. I myself work only alternate weeks, which we call the 'on' weeks. Martin Tomkinson, who joined the 'investigative' staff when Paul Foot left, also works alternate weeks and Patrick Marnham three days in the 'on' week. Other journalists like Gillard, West and Dempster, are regular contributors who come into the office whenever they can find time. Such a system of piece-work has the advantage that it enables the journalists to do other things and prevents us from getting on one another's nerves; the disadvantage is that articles are sometimes written in a hurry without the thoroughness that full-timers backed by large financial resources would be able to devote to their work.

With the more factual material that these journalists were producing there was plainly a greater risk of libel proceedings. It was no longer possible to blur, as one can with satire and parody, the precise meaning of an article; nor could someone under pressure by others to issue a writ dismiss the factual story as 'just a joke'. All the same, the *Eye's* record belies the general impression of constant litigation. Some say that people refrain from suing because they think we have not got any money. There may be something in this. But it is also true that the legal system itself acts as a deterrent, and that many people do not sue because they themselves have not got any money. As well as the high costs of litigation, there is an element of gamble about most cases which applies to both sides. This may explain why, despite several recent awards of over £30,000 in damages, so few libel cases ever come to court. The great majority, not only of *Private Eye's*, are settled on the basis of a printed apology or a statement in open court and the payment of a relatively small sum of damages, sometimes described as 'substantial' to save the plaintiff's face.

Prior to the events described in this book, *Private Eye* had been in court on only four occasions, two of these being in cases

2

brought by one plaintiff, Nora Beloff. In 1963, Lord Russell of Liverpool, author of *The Scourge of the Swastika* and other books about wartime atrocities, sued over an article published a year previously at the time of the trial of Adolf Eichmann. The article described in satirical vein the trial of 'Lord Liver of Cesspool', accused of corrupting millions of readers with his gruesome books. Three years later the case came to court. Russell produced a long line of distinguished witnesses including Sir Charles Petrie and Prof Hugh Trevor-Roper to say that in their view he was a sober and responsible historian. He was awarded £5,000 and, being obviously broke at the time, demanded immediate payment. This was the first occasion on which *Private Eye* launched a libel fund. Peter Cook, who had helped write the Liver of Cesspool piece, organised a charity gala night at the Phoenix Theatre, which raised over half the required sum.

The experience was enough to make me determined in future to settle out of court, which I could have done by paying Russell a much smaller sum than the £5,000 he was awarded by the jury. The case had shown, apart from anything else, just how poor an impression *Private Eye* makes in a court of law. A satirical article which would set the table on a roar across the road in El Vino's takes on a terrible solemnity when read out in the heavy court-room atmosphere. Lawyers sometimes talk of a case being 'laughed out of court' but I have never heard of it being done.

Many people clinging to the old adage, 'the greater the truth, the greater the libel', fail to grasp that if you can show than an article is true, or 'justify' it, as the lawyers say, it is sufficient defence. Even so, the task is not as easy as it sounds. It is one thing to know that something is true, but to be able to prove it to the satisfaction of judge and jury is quite another. Most informants are unlikely to want to step into the witness box and identify themselves.

All the same, there are occasions when even *Private Eye* seems sufficiently equipped with proof to forego the indignity

3

of a grovelling apology and chance its arm in a court action.

In November 1967, the *Eye* published a small 'Colour Section' item about a young Glasgow anarchist called Stuart Christie. Some months previously, Christie had been imprisoned in Spain for carrying explosives. The case created quite a stir, and on his release from prison Christie was approached by the press. He agreed to sell his story to the People in exchange for £600. He returned to Glasgow accompanied by a bodyguard of two *People* reporters, Hugh Farmer and Dennis Cassidy. On their first night in Glasgow, so Christie claimed, the two reporters, after taking part in a TV interview, went off on a pub crawl and ended up in a brothel where they paid for Christie to go to bed with a prostitute.

It was not perhaps a very serious charge to make against two muck-raking journalists. But Farmer and Cassidy, under pressure from their editor Bob Edwards, sued for libel. As the months dragged by they seemed reluctant to go to court. But the *Eye*, and especially Paul Foot who had written the piece, were determined not to settle. We had the evidence not only of Christie, which there seemed no reason to disbelieve, but of two friends of his who had been with him when, three days after the *Eye* article had appeared, he was visited by Cassidy who tried to get him to deny the story. According to both men, Christie joked in the course of this conservation that Cassidy had been too drunk to see a prostitute, to which Cassidy replied 'I wasn't so drunk I didn't see Bollocky Bill [Christie] here performing.'

The case finally came to court before Mr Justice Brabin on 28th January 1969. To our astonishment it opened with Farmer and Cassidy giving a quite different account of what took place on the night of the alleged visit to the brothel. Both maintained that they had accompanied Christie to a pub and then at closing time they drove to a restaurant called the Epicure. Finding, however, that it was full, they settled for a fish and chip shop. At eleven o'clock, they said they went to Scottish Television to watch the transmission of the interview they had made with Christie earlier in the day. They then drove to the Central Hotel for coffee and sandwiches. Their story was confirmed by four witnesses including a journalist who said he met Farmer outside the Central Hotel at midnight, and two employees of Scottish Television who claimed to have met them in the viewing room where they had been given drinks.

This version of events was, as it were, sprung on us in court without any prior warning. All the same, we were able to produce an employee of the Epicure restaurant who pointed out that on the day in question it had been closed because of a public holiday, and also a newsreader from Scottish Television who had been there at the time of the alleged latenight visit and who said it was 'extremely unlikely' that they could have been on the premises without being seen by him.

Despite this evidence the judge found himself unable to discount the evidence of the plaintiffs' witnesses and he ended up awarding Farmer and Cassidy £500 each. *Private Eye* had to pay the costs of the case, including the seven-day court hearing, which amounted to about £10,000. Once again, it seemed, the terrible risks of going to court had been brought home.

One of the *Eye*'s longest and most successful exposures was that of the Poulson affair and the involvement with Poulson of Reginald Maudling at a time when he was Deputy Leader of the Opposition. More damaging to Maudling, however, was another business concern to which he had lent his name, the Real Estate Fund of America, run by an American con-man Jerome Hoffman, subsequently sentenced to a term of imprisonment in America. The story of Maudling's association with Hoffman was of continual interest to Paul Foot and Michael Gillard and led indirectly to our most contracted lawsuit prior to the events described in this book.

Throughout his career, Reginald Maudling, an affable and easy-going politician, enjoyed a close, friendly relationship with the press. But as the *Eye*'s revelations continued, more and more journalists came to believe that there were, to say the least, grounds for disquiet about Maudling's involvement with the Real Estate Fund of America. In early 1971 when Maudling was

5

Home Secretary in a Tory administration, the Business Editor of the *Observer*, Anthony Bambridge, decided that the time had come to investigate the story. But the idea did not appeal to the paper's political correspondent, Miss Nora Beloff, who wrote a long memo to her editor, David Astor, suggesting that she should write an article sympathetic to Maudling. In her memo she described a conversation she had had with Maudling's colleague, William Whitelaw, in which Whitelaw told her, among other things, that Maudling would be the obvious choice for Tory leader should anything happen to Edward Heath.

Beloff won her way, and her apologia for Maudling duly appeared in the *Observer* of 28th February 1971. But in the meantime her memorandum to Astor was leaked to *Private Eye* and included verbatim in the following issue. At the same time we pointed out the numerous errors in her article. Beloff then sued *Private Eye* for breach of copyright i.e. the copyright of the memorandum. (One should add that she also sued for libel over a supposedly jocular reference to her in the same issue by Auberon Waugh, who at that time contributed a political column called 'HP Sauce'.)

Private Eye is used to being sued by journalists. Of all our libel actions I estimate that at least half have been brought by journalists, who tend to be much more sensitive than, say, politicians. But this was the only time that an action for breach of copyright has been brought against us. The only similar case occurred some years ago when Morgan Phillips, the General Secretary of the Labour Party, sued the Guardian for printing an internal memorandum written by him. Phillips, who died before the case could come to court, was advised by the rising young libel lawyer, Arnold Goodman, later to become Chairman of the *Observer*.

The Beloff case lasted for eight days. In defence *Private Eye* made the obvious point that the press, including the *Observer*, were in the habit of regularly printing leaked documents and memoranda. Were Beloff to win, a newspaper would run the risk of a lawsuit on every such occasion. Luckily the *Eye* won, though only, it seemed, on a technicality, since the judge decided that the copyright was not in fact Beloff's and that David Astor who had later assigned it to her was not entitled to do so. The costs of this action alone were over £10,000.

A few months later Beloff won her action against Auberon Waugh's article and was awarded £3,000 by a jury. The *Eye* launched the Ballsoff fund, which raised about £1,000.

One interesting consequence, in this and other cases, was the way in which the plaintiff ended up incurring more odium by going to court than from our publication of the offending piece. Nora Beloff, in particular, became something of a public laughing-stock as a result of her litigation and never quite recovered from it.

Throughout the fifteen years or so of *Private Eye*'s history people often spoke of it as if it was only allowed to exist on sufferance. Sooner or later, surely, someone would come along — the government, perhaps — and finish it off for good. But after some experience of libel actions I failed to see quite how it could be done. Even if someone were to insist on taking a case to court and were to win a huge sum of damages — no one in fact has so far exceeded Lord Russell's £5000 — even then, *Private Eye* would be given time to pay; and in the last resort we would declare ourselves bankrupt and resume publication under another name. Besides which, it was difficult to imagine circumstances in which someone would wish to destroy the magazine altogether.

I was, it turns out, wrong to take so optimistic a view. This book tells the story of what happened when, early in 1976, someone threw the book at *Private Eye* and very nearly finished it off.

7

The Clermont Set

The newspapers of 26 November 1975 carried a bizarre story. The previous day a requiem mass had been held at the Jesuit Church in Farm Street, Mayfair, for Dominic Elwes, a forty-two-year-old playboy and part-time portrait painter who had committed suicide two months previously on 5 September. The requiem had been attended by a number of smart society people as well as members of the deceased's distinguished Catholic family. The speakers at the service were John Aspinall, a professional gambler and former owner of the Clermont Club in Berkeley Square, and Kenneth Tynan, theatre critic and impresario of the pornographic *Oh Calcutta!* In his address Aspinall quoted from Beowulf and referred disparagingly to Elwes's genetic inheritance, which he said had not equipped him to deal with life. This so incensed a young cousin of Elwes's, Tremayne Rodd, that he came up to Aspinall as he left the church and punched him in the face. Aspinall did his best to ignore the attack. 'I'm used to dealing with wild animals,' he said. (In addition to his gambling activities, he runs two zoos in Kent.)

I found this story highly intriguing. I knew enough about the background to realise that it was all in some way linked with the famous Lucan murder case of the previous year. Elwes, I knew, had been a friend of Lucan's. Why had he committed suicide? Why did his death provoke such violent feelings?

An editor's job is not to know stories, so much as to sniff them out. It is a question, as someone has said, of remaining bored until just the right moment. I was not, in November 1975, especially well-informed about the Lucan story. As for Elwes,

I had read about him from time to time in the gossip columns. It was only when the Farm Street incident took place that I thought: 'Something is going on here that may make an interesting article for *Private Eye* '. What it was, or who precisely were the parties involved, I had at that time no clear idea. I knew, however, that it all had something to do with an article about the Lucan case that had appeared in the *Sunday Times Magazine* in June 1975.

Everyone who reads a newspaper will recall the basic facts of that case. On the night of 7 November 1974 Lord Lucan broke into his wife's house and killed his children's nanny under the misapprehension that she was his wife Veronica. After attacking his wife as well, but failing to kill her, he drove off to the house of a friend, Susan Maxwell-Scott, at Uckfield in Sussex. His car was later found at Newhaven. He has never been seen since.

When the murder took place neither the police nor the press knew much about Lucan. He was a rather dim Old Etonian peer, at the time of his disappearance aged forty, whose only interest in life appeared to be gambling. He lived apart from his wife and had recently failed in a High Court action to gain the custody of their two children. Reporters sent to cover the case found it difficult to obtain more information. The reason was simple. Lucan was a man of few friends, but those he had were all members of a small close-knit gambling set centred on the Clermont Club in Berkeley Square. Following the murder they preserved a wall of silence.

It was Elwes who broke ranks, with what were to prove for him fatal results. Some weeks after the murder he was approached by a friend, James Fox, a young Old Etonian journalist on the *Sunday Times*. Fox persuaded Elwes that he intended to write a highly sympathetic account of Lucan's circle for the *Sunday Times Magazine* and Elwes agreed to effect the necessary introductions.

The key figure in what later we came to know as the Lucan set was John Aspinall. The son of an Indian army officer, he was educated at Rugby and Oxford, where he developed a passion for gambling. A highly forceful and energetic character with a magnetic personality, Aspinall, working with his mother Lady Osborne, who was known in gambling circles as 'the Mafia with the handbag' became the chief organiser of smart gambling parties which in the days prior to the Gaming Act of 1960 were illegal. Aspinall was a charming host and provided the right kind of atmosphere in which young men seemed only too keen to squander their fortunes. In 1958 he was sufficiently rich to buy Howletts, a stately home near Canterbury with an estate of fifty-five acres in which he began to build up a large private zoo.

In 1962, two years after gambling was legalised, Aspinall opened the Clermont Club, housed in an elegant eighteenth century building in Berkeley Square designed by William Kent. Here, in the boom years of the sixties, Aspinall came into his own. The building was done up at great expense, all its charming architectural features were preserved. The membership was restricted and gossip columnists were banned. At the rear of the building Aspinall created a small and elegant dining-room looking out on to the little garden. The club had something of the atmosphere of a country house, a home from home for upper-class gamblers. In the basement was the smart night-club Annabel's, run by Aspinall's friend, Mark Birley.

Persuaded by Elwes that James Fox was 'on their side', Aspinall spoke very freely to him about his friend Lucan.

Like all the young aristocrats who got caught in his web, Lord Lucan appealed to both the snob and the businessman in Aspinall. Lucan had worked for about six years in a merchant bank. He gave it up in 1960. Three years later, on the death of his father, he inherited about a quarter of a million pounds. By 1974 he was a virtual bankrupt. His inheritance had been squandered at the Clermont and other gambling clubs. 'I saw in him', Aspinall told Fox, 'a figure like myself, born out of his time. Lucan was a model that would have been better exposed in the early nineteenth century . . . . His qualities as they appeared to me, were the old-fashioned qualities, like loyalty, honesty and reliability.'

It was a curious description to apply to a bankrupt gambler wanted by the police for murder. But to Aspinall, Lucan's homicidal attack was quite pardonable. Like all Lucan's friends, he had nothing but contempt for Lady Lucan. He told Fox how, when questioned by the police investigating the murder, he had said: 'If she'd been my wife I'd have bashed her to death five years before and so would you.' Alone of Lucan's friends, Aspinall was happy to admit that he would have been more than willing to have helped Lucan after the murder, though he denied having done so: 'If a close friend of yours came in covered with blood, having done some frightful deed, the last thing that would have occurred to you is to turn him in.'

For readers of the *Sunday Times* such outspokenness provided something of a sensation. So, too, did the picture Fox gave of some of the political ideas which had developed within the cosy world of the Clermont. The slump of 1973 had rather soured the atmosphere there, and Lucan's own ideas had become more and more right-wing. Searching for clues, police had found records of Hitler's speeches in his flat.

As for Aspinall, he had always subscribed to extreme right-wing views of a romantic and snobbish kind. His philosophy, and that of his circle as a whole, had been greatly influenced by his friend from Oxford days, Edward — known as Teddy — Goldsmith who, with the help of his wealthy brother Jimmy, had founded the *Ecologist* magazine in 1970. Two years later, Goldsmith produced a special issue of the paper called *Blueprint for Survival*, which was republished by Penguin with the blessing of a number of distinguished scientists and laymen including Sir Julian Huxley, Sir Peter Medawar and Peter Scott. It was an apocalyptic tract, prophesying, and to a great extent welcoming, the imminent collapse of industrial society. Goldsmith and his colleagues advocated the need for a return to smaller self-sufficient communities, relying on natural energy, sewage etc. Quite how this desirable goal was to be achieved

11

was never adequately explained, though as a pre-requisite to the new era, the *Blueprint* called for an immediate cut in the birth rate, to be achieved if necessary by compulsory birth control and abortion.

Aspinall enthusiastically took up these ideas and began to refer to his fellow Londoners as 'the urban bio-mass'. Launching the *Blueprint* from the Clermont Club, he said he welcomed the recent floods in Bangladesh which had swept away thousands of human beings. 'Gambler that I have always been,' he wrote, 'brave man that I am, I tremble before the oncoming storm.'

Meanwhile Teddy Goldsmith had retired in 1972 to a commune in Cornwall, where he tried rather unsuccessfully to practise self-sufficiency by breeding exotic chickens. In the fastness of the West Country his thoughts reverted to his Stone Age ancestors and he became convinced that a study of their way of life could provide many of the answers to twentieth-century problems, whereas Aspinall, an amateur biologist, looked even further back in time, to the apes. *Homo sapiens*, he concluded, was a thoroughly degenerate species. If man was to redeem himself, he had somehow to recapture the order and discipline which were to be observed in animal communities.

Such ideas seem altogether too bizarre to be taken seriously. But one man in particular had been entranced by the world of the Clermont, regarding its habitués as a glittering circle and the club itself as a little oasis of civilisation in a hostile world. Dominic Elwes was often spoken of as the court jester of the Clermont set. A man of undoubted charm, he was a brilliant conversationalist and story teller to whom, it was said, even Peter Ustinov bowed the knee. Born in 1931, the son of the portrait painter Simon Elwes, he was brought up as a Catholic and educated at Downside. But from the beginning, nothing went right for him. He was expelled from school. (One of the monks later told Auberon Waugh that Elwes was the only pupil he had known who was possessed by the devil.) At the age of sixteen he joined the army but was dismissed before he could gain a commission. In society circles Elwes had the reputation of the traditional bounder. He was the sort of man who was always being physically ejected from debutante dances. In 1958 he became notorious when he eloped with a nineteen-year-old heiress, Tessa Kennedy. They married in Cuba but were divorced eleven years later.

Elwes tried his hand at many things, but with no success. He painted portraits for the upper classes; he worked on *Topic*, the short-lived news magazine launched in 1963. He even tried to become a Liberal candidate. Although he was never a real gambler like Lucan, he was nearly always broke. He relied in every way on wealthy friends to keep him going. Such reliance was not really to do with money. Elwes loved the world of the Clermont and Annabel's and was pathetically convinced that James Fox, who came from the right sort of background, would share his enthusiasm.

So when he was offered £200 by the *Sunday Times* — 'Sorely needed. Sorely needed', he told Nigel Dempster — Elwes agreed without hesitation to execute an oil painting of the lunchtime scene at the Clermont to go with Fox's article about the Lucan set. He had to work in a hurry and the picture had a primitive look about it. He could not quite capture the waiter, and turned the figure instead into a rear view of Nicholas Soames, son of Sir Christopher Soames, a huge ape-like figure in the corner. Despite its crudity, however, the painting conveyed vividly the doom-laden atmosphere in the little William Kent dining-room, with the group of friends seated at the long table—Lucan, Aspinall, Lucan's stockbroking friend Stephen Raphael, the Earl of Suffolk and Berkshire, Charles Benson, Peter West and, in the foreground, his hand imperiously raised to summon a waiter, the millionaire food tycoon, Jimmy Goldsmith.

The Eye Investigates

It was on the Monday following the Elwes memorial service that I went up to London. That morning I rang Nigel Dempster at his office at the *Daily Mail*.

Dempster, the best known of a new generation of gossip columnists and a contributor to *Private Eye* since 1968, has an encyclopaedic knowledge of high society. If anyone was likely to know about the Lucan world, it was Dempster. But I had another reason for ringing him. I knew that he had been a friend of Dominic Elwes and therefore would have followed the extraordinary sequence of events since the publication of James Fox's article on 8 June 1975.

The article had caused a minor sensation in the Clermont. In spite of Elwes's predictions, Fox had quite failed to appreciate his civilised and witty friends. On the contrary, they came over as a group of weird and thoroughly unpleasant people. Hitherto public opinion, fed by wild rumours, had taken Lucan's side. Fox, however, made Lucan the villain of the story and his wife a pathetic victim who, though her own snobbery was partly to blame, had been ganged up on by a group of sinister eccentrics. Rumour had it that Lady Lucan was mad: Fox showed that most of the real madness was on the other side.

One man in particular took offence, not only at what Fox had written but at the many garish photographs which were used to illustrate the article. This was Jimmy Goldsmith.

Goldsmith, a founder-member of the Clermont circle, was one of Aspinall's oldest and closest friends. Expelled from Eton at the age of 16, son of a rich hotelier in France, he had drifted into the gambling world of the early fifties, where Aspinall and his mother held sway. But unlike Lucan and Elwes, Goldsmith had since prospered. Following the launching of his grocery business, Cavenham, in the early sixties, Goldsmith had become a highly successful and powerful tycoon. Aspinall, having carefully studied the power structure of his treasured collection of gorillas, eventually yielded to Goldsmith the place of honour at the head of the Clermont table. Goldsmith was now more powerful and should therefore become leader of the pack.

It was in this capacity that, following the publication of the *Sunday Times* article, Goldsmith gave orders that Dominic Elwes was henceforth to be banished. Not only had Elwes betrayed the confidences of the club; he had also, Goldsmith claimed, sold photographs to the *Sunday Times*. These included a sequence of colour pictures taken at a Goldsmith house party in Acapulco in March 1973. One of them, showing Goldsmith's mistress Annabel Birley with her arm draped affectionately round Lucan's shoulder, had been published on the cover of the magazine.

Why Goldsmith reacted so angrily was not explained until much later. At any rate, Elwes, who vehemently denied having sold the pictures to the *Sunday Times*, found the doors literally barred to him at his two favourite haunts, Annabel's, the nightclub below the Clermont, and Mark's, the restaurant in nearby Charles Street. Waiters were given orders not to serve him. But far worse was to be deprived of the company of his friends, especially that of Goldsmith, whom he idolised. From that moment on, Elwes, already in bad shape, began to deteriorate. On 20 June, twelve days after the publication of Fox's article, he left England for Nice to stay in a flat belonging to his friend, Earl Compton. At Heathrow Airport he happened to meet Nigel Dempster. Elwes poured out the story of the photographs and how he was being wrongly blamed for selling them. He burst into tears. Dempster there and then rang Goldsmith at his office, but Goldsmith refused to speak to him. Dempster then left a message with Goldsmith's secretary to the effect that Elwes had nothing whatever to do with the sale of the photographs. There was never any reply.

From Nice, Elwes travelled to Cuarton, near Algeciras in Southern Spain, where he had an interest in a property development. At Cuarton, he met Nicholas Luard, an old friend and one-time co-owner with Peter Cook of *Private Eye*. Luard later described for me his impressions of this encounter, for possible use in our defence:

> 'We arrived at a neighbour's house for dinner to find Elwes among the guests. It turned out he had arrived a few hours earlier and was staying in the house of a close friend of ours, Milet Delme-Radcliffe, half a mile away.
>
> The last time I'd seen him was in London six months earlier. Then he'd been his usual self — energetic, laughing, ebullient, telling the anecdotes that rightly gave him an almost legendary reputation as a raconteur. The difference on this occasion was extraordinary.
>
> He was trembling, stuttering, rambling, almost incoherent. He was unable to eat, he had to be helped down steps, he kept dropping glasses.
>
> Elwes stayed at Cuarton for about a month. He had two obsessions in conversation: Lucan and Goldsmith. Whatever sympathy he might have had for Lucan at the start had long since vanished. He blamed Lucan for what Goldsmith was doing to him, remained convinced that Lucan was still alive and clung to the hope that he would reappear in the hope that this would somehow change Goldsmith's attitude.'

Elwes returned to London at the end of August. He had nothing left to live for. His mother was in a psychiatric home, his father was dying. What little money he had had been invested in a disastrous bank, Morris Wigram. On 5 September, his body was found by a girlfriend, Melissa Wyndham, in his small flat off the King's Road. He had taken an overdose of barbiturates. A *Times* article prophesying economic doom and written by his friend, Peter Jay, was pinned to the wall. He left a long rambling note containing many religious passages. In another, shorter note he said: 'I curse Mark [Birley] and Jimmy [Goldsmith] from beyond the grave. I hope they are happy now.'

This was the story that Dempster told me in outline. He himself was due to travel to India that weekend, but before he left he wrote a memorandum in which he set out all that he knew about what had happened. I had already asked Patrick Marnham to write a long piece on the affair for *Private Eye*. Originally our intention was to do no more than provide a sequel to James Fox's *Sunday Times* article but after reading Dempster's draft, it struck me that the story was a rather more significant one than I had at first thought. The reason was the involvement of Jimmy Goldsmith. Goldsmith was more than just a rich gambler. Only two months previously he had, with the approval of the Bank of England, taken over the chairmanship of Slater Walker from his friend, Jim Slater.

Jim Slater had resigned from the chairmanship of Slater Walker on 24 October 1975, thus bringing an end to his career as the biggest financial 'whizz-kid' of the sixties. His resignation, amid stories of corruption in the Far East, left the City in a state of shock and confusion, for in his heyday Slater had controlled a huge financial empire engaged in banking, property, investment, and insurance. In order to prevent overseas loss of confidence in the City, the Bank of England now felt obliged to step in and save Slater Walker — at a cost, it later emerged, of £110,000,000 of public money. As part of the rescue operation Goldsmith had agreed to take over as Chairman.

It is often left to *Private Eye* to ask the awkward question. So now it struck me as rather extraordinary that the friend of Aspinall and Lucan, the hounder of Elwes, should be brought in to restore confidence as the saviour of Slater Walker with the backing and blessing of the Bank of England. I told Marnham, therefore, to concentrate his article on Goldsmith, including a review of his financial career. Marnham had a long talk with

James Fox. But, unfortunately, Michael Gillard, *Private Eye's* expert on financial matters, was in Manchester, having just returned from abroad, and was therefore only able to supply an outline of Goldsmith's business career.

All the same, with the material provided by Fox and Dempster, there was quite enough to go on. Under the heading 'All's Well That Ends Elwes', Marnham began by recapitulating the Fox story. 'From the beginning,' he wrote, 'the police have met obstruction and silence from the circle of gamblers and boneheads with whom Lord Lucan and Dominic Elwes associated.' According to Fox, on the day after the Lucan murder, a lunch had been held at Aspinall's house in London. Present were a group of Lucan's closest friends, including Goldsmith and Elwes. The idea was to discuss what they should do about 'Lucky', as he was known, if necessary to help him. Not all of them at that stage could believe that Lucan was guilty of murder. The important thing was to speak to Veronica Lucan, now in hospital, to find out what had happened and, in particular, how much she had told the police. Accordingly, following the lunch, Elwes, who was on better terms with Lady Lucan than anyone else present was 'sent down' — or so the *Private Eye* article said — to St. George's Hospital to find out the answers to these questions.

Fox had merely stated that Goldsmith had been one of those present at the lunch. But did it not follow, given his status as the richest and most powerful of the friends, that he would have taken the chair? And did it not also follow that it would have been on Goldsmith's instructions that Elwes went to the hospital?

So, at least, we thought at *Private Eye*. And there was another point to link Goldsmith with the case. Greville Howard, an Old Etonian backgammon player and frequenter of the Clermont club, would have been a crucial witness on the inquest of the murdered nanny, Sandra Rivert, in June. Howard had already told the police of a discussion with Lucan some weeks before the murder in which Lucan spoke of his intention to kill his

18

wife. Howard had been in a private clinic, the Nuffield, under-going treatment for a bad back.

'When he is feeling stronger [Marnham wrote in the *Private Eye* article] Greville Howard works for Goldsmith at Slater Walker, which the latter has taken over follow-ing the early retirement of Jim Slater. [Howard had also, though we did not know it at the time, worked as Goldsmith's Personal Assistant at Cavenham during 1970-71.] Before this, Goldsmith made his fortune with Caven-ham Foods and Anglo-Continental Investment. He is a cousin of the French Rothschilds and is known for his ability in dressing up the balance sheets of his various companies with house deals whereby large sums are transferred from one company to another for purposes which are not altogether clear to outsiders. During the great stock-market boom of 1972-73, Cavenham's share-price was miles above its asset level, as the *Sunday Times Business News* pointed out. Goldsmith reacted by trying to suppress the story on the strength of his joint business interests with Lord Thomson, but this did not work. He has now taken to issuing solicitors letters to unfriendly papers, and has instructed the *Sunday Times* not to men-tion his name again without first communicating with his solicitor.' [This was a small but insignificant mistake. It was the *Daily Express* that had been so instructed.]

There then followed an account of the Elwes story, and the article ended: 'Given the vote of confidence which the City has recently given Jimmy, he probably is quite happy, and there seems to be no reason to question the Bank of England's stated confidence in him as a man of integrity, well fitted to guide the helm of a great public enterprise.'

In spite of the rather frantic conditions in which it was put together, I counted the article a success, though I would have liked it to have included more details of Goldsmith's involvement with Slater Walker. It was soon possible, however, to remedy this omission. By the time the next issue of *Private Eye* went to press, Michael Gillard was back in action.

Gillard has contributed items to the 'Slicker' column of *Private Eye* since 1969, when he was working for the 'City Page' of the *Daily Express*. In 1972 he was paid £10,000 to leave the *Daily Express* after embarrassing the then Chairman, Sir Max Aitken, by describing the head of the South African tobacco company, Rothmans, Dr Anton Rupert, as 'a friend of South African Prime Minister John Vorster and cash backer of the ruling Nationalist Party'. (Rupert, also a member of the Afrikaner Broederbond secret society, was highly embarrassed by the revelation as Rothmans had dealings in many African countries hostile to South Africa.) Since then, Gillard has worked for Granada's *World in Action* programme. Meanwhile, even the *Eye*'s strongest opponents have been forced to acknowledge that the 'Slicker' column is consistently accurate, besides being invariably ahead of the field.

Gillard had been among the first to point out that Slater had feet of straw, at a time when Fleet Street was singing his praises. Now I asked him to turn his attention to Slater's successor. He began in the following issue of the *Eye* by examining a statement that Goldsmith had made to the *Financial Times* on taking over as Chairman of Slater Walker: 'I am sure that two new boards, neither of them linked to the past, can see the thing in proper commercial perspective.' This statement seemed to imply that Goldsmith himself had no links with the past, i.e. with Slater. But this was far from being the case. Goldsmith and Slater were not only close friends — Slater, being a keen backgammon-player, frequented the Clermont Club and was rumoured to have lent half a million pounds to John Aspinall — their companies were also linked in a variety of ways and Goldsmith's companies were major shareholders in Slater Walker. 'It is legitimate to query', Gillard wrote, after detailing the Goldsmith/Slater connections, 'whether in view of the close personal and corporate involvement, Goldsmith is the most independent chairman . . .'

Meanwhile Gillard had unearthed an additional item of interest concerning Goldsmith's legal advisor, Eric Levine. Levine, who was not only Goldsmith's solicitor but a director of two of his companies, had been closely involved, though in no criminal capacity, with T. Dan Smith, who by now was serving a prison sentence for his part in corrupting local councillors in the north-east of England. Levine had been Smith's lawyer, had helped to form Vinleigh, a PR company used by Smith to pay bribes, and had also been a director of Tyne-Tees Television in 1968 along with Smith.

The 'Slicker' column of 9 January 1976 detailed these facts, referring to 'an intriguing link', i.e. Levine, between T. Dan Smith and Goldsmith.

At no time during this period was I conscious that we were doing anything special or taking any particular risk with regard to libel. Goldsmith was certainly a new target for *Private Eye*, but he had been mentioned before, usually in the gossip column or in 'Slicker'.

It therefore came as something of a surprise when on 12 January, three days after the issue containing the Levine article was published, Goldsmith issued sixty-three writs, against *Private Eye* and over thirty of our distributors, and applied to the High Court to bring proceedings for Criminal Libel in respect of the Elwes article.

Here Comes the Judge

Looking back, it seems remarkable how little we were concerned at the time. The unparalleled quantity of writs, the introduction of Criminal Libel — an offence carrying a prison sentence, something unheard of in recent times — made the whole thing seem rather absurd. I myself had arranged to take an issue of *Private Eye* off to finish a book I was writing. I retired to the country and was, so far as I can remember, well able to dismiss James Goldsmith from my mind.

But when I returned I found that at least one matter required urgent attention. Goldsmith had sued thirty-seven of our distributors — wholesalers and retailers — for handling the issues which mentioned Slater Walker and Levine. Following the writs had come a letter from Eric Levine himself containing a strongly implied threat that Criminal Libel proceedings would be launched against these firms unless they ceased to distribute *Private Eye*.

David Cash, the *Eye*'s Business Manager, had called a meeting on the day I got back to try to reassure the distributors. They were mostly small businessmen and few of them had seen a libel writ before. With the help of our solicitor, Geoffrey Bindman, we tried to convince them that there was nothing to worry about. *Private Eye* would indemnify them against any damages. I remember saying that as far as I was concerned it was just another libel action. At the time I meant it.

Sixteen agreed not to sell *Private Eye* and at the end of the day, out of the thirty-seven, seventeen decided to fight the action. In the process *Private Eye* lost 12,000 copies out of a circulation standing at that time at about 100,000.

Now came an even more serious blow. Goldsmith had sworn an affidavit on 2 February setting out what he considered to be the Criminal Libel. Curiously, he ignored completely the Elwes side of the story, which implied that he had helped to hound Elwes to death, and complained only of the introductory paragraphs dealing with the Lucan murder. These, he claimed, suggested:

'(i) that there was a conspiracy amongst a group of Lord Lucan's friends, described in the article as the 'Lucan circle', firstly to obstruct the course of justice and secondly to assist the 'fugitive Earl';

(ii) that I was the richest and most powerful member of that group and played a leading and dominant part in the conspiracy;

(iii) that because of my dominance and wealth and because of his fear of me Mr Dominic Elwes was compelled against his will to visit Lady Lucan in hospital and to discover what she had told the police who were enquiring into the death of Sandra Rivett

(iv) that Mr Greville Howard was deliberately evading giving evidence at the inquest of Sandra Rivett and that such evasion was due to pressure and persuasion on my part.'

Goldsmith now played his trump card. He had not, he said — and he was unlikely to say it if it was untrue — been present at the lunch at Aspinall's house on the day after the murder. James Fox had made a mistake in his *Sunday Times* article. It emerged that at the time Goldsmith had wished to sue the *Sunday Times* but had been restrained by counsel and contented himself with a strongly-worded letter of complaint to the paper. The editor acknowledged privately that there had been an error. As Fox had made no great play of Goldsmith's presence at the lunch — it was our assumption that, had he been there, as Fox said, he would have taken charge — the paper did not regard it as a very serious affair, and Fox himself, who had gone abroad after writing his piece, knew nothing about his mistake or its consequences.

From our point of view, however, it was crucial. Marnham's description of the events after Lucan's disappearance hinged on the lunch. Goldsmith's attendance was in fact the only thing to connect him directly with any 'conspiracy' or with Elwes's visit to the hospital. Our QC, Michael Kempster, who had acted for *Private Eye* in the two Beloff actions, took a rather gloomy view of the defence. He thought it possible for Goldsmith to substantiate the conspiracy charge. There was, for example, our use of the word 'obstruction', an interesting example of the way in which a single word can alter the libellous connotations of an article. 'From the beginning,' Marnham had written, 'the police have met *obstruction* [my italics] and silence from the circle of gamblers and boneheads . . .' Of course, 'obstructing the police in their enquiries' is a criminal offence; yet we had not intended to suggest any criminality. An expression like 'non-co-operation' would have done just as well and might have made it more difficult for Goldsmith to formulate his charge.

Since the Lord Russell of Liverpool case we had employed a barrister to come in on press day and read the back pages and the 'Colour Section' for libel. At the time of the Goldsmith affair we relied on several different lawyers and the benefits of being read for libel were not always apparent. In most cases where material is obviously risky, what one wants to know is not whether an article is defamatory but whether the person defamed is likely to sue — something that a lawyer cannot be expected to assess. There are occasions, however, when small changes in the wording can take the sting out of an article. On the libel reader's advice I had toned down at least one passage in Marnham's piece, but the 'obstruction' point was one which we both overlooked.

On purely legal grounds, Kempster was more confident. Under the Law of Libel Amendment Act of 1888, brought in to put an end to a spate of frivolous prosecutions, Goldsmith had to apply to a High Court judge for leave to bring a Criminal Libel action. The hearing was not due until the beginning of April. According to Kempster, Goldsmith was very unlikely to succeed.

In the meantime I was visited at *Private Eye* by an emissary from Jim Slater, in the shape of his close friend and supporter through thick and thin, Mr Patrick Hutber, the City Editor of the *Sunday Telegraph*. Slater, he said, was worried about his friend Jimmy Goldsmith. Goldsmith was a manic depressive who was prone to go off the deep end from time to time. When cast in gloom, Hutber said, Goldsmith liked to restore his morale by spending a week or so in a fascist country. The trouble was that they were getting more and more difficult to find, what with the overthrow of the Greek colonels and the death of General Franco. Meanwhile, Slater was most anxious to see if there was not some way of settling the dispute between Jimmy and *Private Eye*.

I remember answering confidently that I myself was not in the least bit worried. No one thought Goldsmith had a hope of getting his Criminal Libel action off the ground. Hutber, with some prescience, replied that I ought to know by now that lawyers' forecasts often turned out to be disastrously wrong, and left looking downcast, his mission unfulfilled.

The Criminal Libel action was due to be heard by Mr Justice Chapman on 8 April. But, as often seems to happen, all parties trooped into court only to find that there had been a mix-up. The lawyers put their heads together and decided that Chapman's timetable could not accommodate the hearing. It was postponed until the 13th when it would be heard by another judge. The change may well have affected the whole course of what followed.

A few days before the case was due to be heard, our solicitor Geoffrey Bindman, acting on Michael Kempster's advice and with my approval, sent the following letter to Goldsmith's solicitor:

'Our clients have carefully studied Mr Goldsmith's

affidavit and in the light of its contents they are satisfied that there could be no truth in the suggestion that Mr Goldsmith was a party to an attempt to obstruct the police in investigating the murder of Lord Lucan [*sic*]. Any imputation to the contrary which the article of 12 December 1975 may have borne arose from our client's honestly held belief that your client was present at a lunch given by Mr John Aspinall on the day after the murder of Mrs Sandra Rivett. In this they now accept that they were mistaken. We therefore write to say that our clients withdraw and apologise for this allegation. We leave it to you to decide how this apology and withdrawal can be made public.'

But the letter received no reply. *Private Eye*, it appeared, was now to make another of its rare excursions into court, and in this case the law itself was both exotic and obscure.

The offence of Criminal Libel dates back to the days of the sixteenth century when, according to J.R. Spencer in a recent and informative survey in the *Criminal Law Review* (July 1977), 'the Star Chamber regarded with the deepest suspicion the printed word in general, and anything which looked like criticism of the established institutions of Church and State in particular'. Offenders were liable to the severest penalties. The Puritan agitator William Prynne (1600-1669) had his ear cut off and was branded on both cheeks with the letters SL — standing for Seditious Libeller. Until the nineteenth century, governments made regular use of the law as a convenient means of punishing those who were thought top be subversive or revolutionary in their aims. John Wilkes was prosecuted for Criminal Libel, and in the following century William Cobbett was sentenced to two years' imprisonment in 1809. Leigh Hunt was also jailed for describing the Prince Regent as 'a fat Adonis of fifty'. Many lesser known figures suffered a similar fate. But in later years, following the Reform Bill of 1832, the number of political prosecutions declined, and the most recent case appears to be that of a left-wing journalist called Mylius, who, in 1911, accused George V of being a bigamist.

Meanwhile, however, it was always possible for individual citizens to institute proceedings against their fellows, and there were several well-known cases of this kind, especially in the nineteenth century — the most famous being that of Oscar Wilde, who, in 1895, brought a prosecution against the Marquess of Queensbury who had accused him on a card delivered to his club of 'posing as a Sodomite'. (The prosecution failed and led eventually to Wilde's own downfall.) Cases of this kind, however, had also declined in modern times, partly as a result of the previously mentioned amendment to the law in 1888 which made it necessary for the plaintiff to get permission from a High Court judge before bringing a prosecution against a newspaper. Though there was a continuing trickle of cases brought against individuals — a man was sentenced to six months' imprisonment in 1971 for libelling a policeman — the most recently recorded case of an editor being sued appeared to be that of Lord Alfred Douglas, who, in 1923, accused Winston Churchill of deliberately losing the Battle of Jutland in order to cash in on some shares on the American stockmarket. Churchill sued for Criminal Libel and Douglas was given six months.

Though English laws fall into desuetude, they are seldom repealed until they prove an embarrassment. They remain on the statute book like rusting old weapons in an armoury. Lawyers sometimes take the view that it would be a mistake to do away with them, simply on the basis that you never know when they might come in handy. Thus, when Mr Justice Faulks conducted his enquiry into the law of defamation in 1975 he recommended that the Criminal Libel laws should be maintained, even though he acknowledged that it was seldom used and served only a very limited purpose.

This, then, was the law we were up against, and the hearing finally came up at the Law Courts in the Strand before Mr Justice Wien on 13 April. Proceedings were *in camera*. Goldsmith had retained two QCs. The first, Mr Lewis Hawser, did all the talking while the second, Mr A.T. Hoolahan, sat on the bench behind him apparently doing very little. This was also the first opportunity I had had to observe Goldsmith's solicitor, Eric Levine — a small, insignificant figure, very smartly dressed. My impression, I remember, was that of a servant quietly carrying out his master's orders. Goldsmith himself did not come to court.

Over the following months we were all to become more than familiar with the figure of Mr Lewis Hawser, QC. The brother of the theatrical producer Frank Hauser — Lewis anglicised the name — Hawser came, like Mr Justice Wien, from a Cardiff Jewish background. If Queen's Counsel were to be put into divisions like boxers, Hawser would be a heavyweight. A tall, lugubrious looking man with a sonorous voice, he believed in piling up every single point that might possibly be in his client's favour, regardless of the atmosphere in the courtroom. This bulldozer technique, infuriating as it might be to some of his listeners, was often very effective. He began on this, as on every subsequent occasion, with a long catalogue of Goldsmith's offices. 'My client is Chairman of Cavenham, one of the largest industrial companies in Britain . . . In France, Generale Alimentaire . . . In Sweden, AB Felix, the second largest food company . . . In Spain . . .' And so on, and so on. 'His honesty and integrity,' Hawser intoned, 'are of vital concern to many thousands of the public, his employees, shareholders or investors, and to numerous great financial institutions headed by the Bank of England.' And this pillar of society, he went on, had been subjected by *Private Eye* to a 'campaign of vilification', almost, it seemed, unparalleled in the long history of the press — at which point, I thought, Hawser made a bad mistake. For he proceeded to read out a sheaf of cuttings, detailing every single reference that there had ever been to Goldsmith in *Private Eye*, many of them small and insignificant references in the 'Grovel' column to his private life. Unless all of them were untrue, which was unlikely, the cumulative effect was to suggest a very different picture from the man of impeccable respectability that Hawser had described in his opening. Quite apart from his friendship with people such as Lucan and Slater, Goldsmith was, it seemed, an inveterate gambler who kept a wife and family in France and a mistress and a family in England.

Michael Kempster, replying for the *Eye*, relied heavily on a purely legal defence. There had been no prosecutions against newspapers in recent years, and there was no reason to begin now. As for Criminal Libel itself, he quoted a number of authorities, for example the famous Chief Justice, Lord Coleridge, who had said:

> 'There ought to be some public interest concerned, something affecting the Crown or the guardians of the public peace (likely to be broken by the alleged libel), to justify the recourse by a private person to a criminal remedy by way of indictment. If either by reason of the continued reputation or infamous character of the libel, breach of the peace is likely to ensure, then the libeller should be indicted; but in the absence of any such conditions, the personal squabble between two private individuals ought not to be permitted by sound law to be the subject of a criminal indictment.'

Mr Justice Wien started to sum up on the morning of the second day. Listening to a judge summing up always reminds me of watching the little white ball whizzing round on a roulette wheel. It seems a matter of pure chance whether it will land on the red or the black. But the longer Wien continued, the more certain I became that Goldsmith had failed. He seemed so reluctant to set a Criminal Libel prosecution in motion after a gap of so many years. He was concerned that there was no appeal against his judgement.

Wien had another difficulty to contend with. There had been a tradition that what made a Criminal Libel different from an ordinary civil one was that it was so serious as to be likely to provoke a breach of the peace; in other words, the person libelled would be sufficiently outraged that he would be likely to take the law into his own hands. Such a definition was, of course, extremely vague, but it at least provided judges with some kind of criterion in deciding whether cases should proceed. However, in a case in 1936, *R v Wicks*, the judge had ruled that it was not a necessary ingredient of the offence that 'the libel in question would have been unusually likely to provoke the wrath of the person defamed'. This ruling had therefore done away with the breach of the peace criterion and had left open the question of how one defined a Criminal Libel and what made it different from an ordinary one.

As Wien progressed, therefore, I became more and more convinced that he would throw out the application. But as he neared his conclusion, he seemed to change tack. He took Lord Coleridge's criteria and applied them to the present case. Coleridge had said there ought to be a matter of public interest. So there was.

> 'Where a person occupies the position that Mr Goldsmith does, it can become a matter of public importance, and it can well become a matter of public importance when there is an association with the Bank of England and where his integrity has been impugned and a criminal offence has been alleged against him and so far nothing has been made public about the matter and where, in particular, a campaign of vilification goes on for month after month with no let-up, not even after it was known that this application was going to be made.'

He paused, looked around the court, and then announced: 'I have come to the conclusion that the public interest requires the institution of criminal proceedings.'

To say that my heart sank sounds melodramatic. But something of the kind occurred. What no one had thought possible had come to pass. We had all been treating it almost as a joke, and now I was going to be charged with a criminal offence with the possibility of a prison sentence at the end of it. Outside the courtroom I looked for our QC, Michael Kempster, but he had gone. Geoffrey Bindman, our solicitor, was as surprised as I was. He said *Private Eye* must immediately start a libel fund. Hawser and Levine were plainly jubilant.

When I got back to *Private Eye* there was another surprise in store for me. 'Tiny' Rowland, Chairman of the huge mining conglomerate Lonrho, wanted me to ring him. I dialled the Lonrho offices and asked to speak to the Chairman. 'Mr Ingrams,' he said, 'I've just heard about the case on the lunchtime news. I want to offer you my support. There will be no quid pro quo. You must go on writing about me whenever you want. You can have £5,000 — whatever you want.'

I managed to stutter out my thanks.

From Marzipan to Ermine

Lawyers are very like doctors, and the difference between a solicitor and a barrister is similar to that between a GP and the specialist or hospital consultant. The similarity extends to the formalities with which barristers conduct their business and the many subtle ways in which they contrive to overawe their clients. Visiting a barrister in the cloistered calm of one of the Inns of Court, you announce your presence to a clerk who asks you to take a seat in a book-lined waiting room. After a suitable interval, you and your solicitor will be ushered into the barrister's room. Sometimes the barrister, like the consultant, has students with him sitting in on the proceedings, taking notes. From his safe position behind his imposing desk, the barrister eventually gives his diagnosis.

Most consultations are conducted with a junior. But as a case nears the courtroom, a QC has to be briefed. Because of his seniority he tends to be an even more imposing figure, to whom the solicitor and the junior are bound to defer. It is very hard in these circumstances for the client to impose his view of the case. For a start he probably has little or no legal knowledge and almost certainly no experience of the courts. When a QC, therefore, gives his opinion of what is or is not likely to impress a judge, it is very difficult for the client to disagree. In nine cases out of ten, he ends up putting himself in the hands of the lawyers. In the circumstances, he has very little alternative.

Before the case I had never thought to question Michael Kempster's handling of our defence. It was only after Mr Justice Wien had reached his verdict and I went home and thought about it that I realised what an elementary tactical blunder we had made by admitting the conspiracy allegation and apologising to Goldsmith for it in advance. Certainly it was true that Goldsmith had not been present at Aspinall's lunch. It was true that there was nothing to link him with a conspiracy to obstruct the police, even if there was a conspiracy. But to admit as much was like showing Goldsmith at the start of a poker game that we had no cards whatever in our hand and then going on to play the game. Kempster had admitted that *Private Eye* had no defence in a Criminal Libel case in the hope that it would influence the judge in our favour. Wien, however, seized on the point as all the more reason for the case to proceed.

Like so many moves in the legal game, this again was one that had been agreed at the last minute and without any proper consultation. Looking back, it seemed an obvious mistake, but at the time, it should be remembered, none of us thought that Goldsmith had a hope of launching a Criminal Libel case. There was some logic, therefore, in assuming that he would have even less hope if the *Eye* admitted its errors at the start — though even then we left ourselves open to a civil action, which Goldsmith was perfectly entitled to bring and which could well be financially more damaging to *Private Eye* than a criminal prosecution, as the damages were more likely to exceed the fine.

At any rate, my immediate mood was one of intense despondency. When I got home I telephoned a barrister friend to ask his advice. He arranged to meet me in The Bull at Streatley. Over lunch we discussed the case. He advised me that my best course was to try to reach an out-of-court settlement with Goldsmith. Failing that, we could still fight the case by challenging the judgement in *R v Wicks*; in other words we could try to maintain that, despite what a judge had ruled in 1936, there did have to be a possibility of a breach of the peace for the libel to be criminal. But this might mean going to the House of Lords, and it was bound to be expensive. So all in all, my friend concluded, an out-of-court settlement was the best that we could hope for. I asked him who he would recommend to fight the action in the place of Michael Kempster. He suggested three QCs, the first of whom was James Comyn. The name meant nothing to me.

It was Easter that weekend. On the following Tuesday I went back to the office to find a changed atmosphere. Up until Wien's verdict it had been a phoney war. Now we had to take Goldsmith seriously. The readers had already sent in money spontaneously for what we were about to christen 'The Goldenballs Fund', after Gillard's nickname for Goldsmith.

There was support of other kinds, too. *The Times* printed a number of letters attacking Wien's decision, including a long one from Lord Shawcross. MPs were putting down questions to the Attorney General, asking him if he would take over the case, as he was entitled to do, and quash it. Mr Silkin, however, refused. Journalist friends everywhere offered support and we decided at once to do everything possible to strengthen our hands in the Slater Walker and Levine actions.

Another matter of urgency was to find out everything we could about Goldsmith and what he was up to. Over the ensuing months a mass of material was collected and this is the rough picture that emerged.

James Goldsmith was forty-three, a millionaire. The most obvious thing about him was that he was, like his business, cosmopolitan, a genuine multi-national. His grandfather was a German Jew, his mother a French Catholic; his wife, too, was French, and lived in France with their children. He had a half-Bolivian daughter from his first marriage. He also had an English mistress, Lady Annabel Birley, by whom he had two young children, Jemima and Zacharias. He lived a double life — weekdays in London, office in the City, house in Regent's Park; weekends in Paris, mansion on the Left Bank.

This rootlessness, the lack of any proper home, was something Goldsmith had known all his life. His father, too, had had a dual nationality. The son of a Jewish immigrant from Frankfurt, Major Frank Goldsmith started off by integrating himself thoroughly in English society. He acquired a country home called Cavenham in Suffolk and became the Tory MP for Stowmarket. But, after the First World War, he moved to France and went into the hotel business. A well-liked figure, known as 'Monsieur le Major', he became eventually the owner of a chain of hotels in England and France, including the Carlton at Cannes and the Scribe in Paris.

At a late age, the Major married a French girl described by her own son, Jimmy, as 'a peasant from the Auvergne'. There were two sons of the marriage. Teddy, the elder, went to Eton and Oxford; Jimmy was born on 26 February 1933, when his father was fifty-five. He described himself as 'an afterthought'.

The Goldsmith parents had no fixed home and Jimmy was brought up in the foyers of his father's hotels in an atmosphere of loose women and bouncing cheques. In 1945 he was sent to Eton, like his brother, but 'resigned' — to use his own expression — when he was still only sixteen. Later he gave as a reason the fact that he had won £8,000 in a betting coup at Lewes, but though the story of the bet is probably true, it is likely that he left school for more conventional reasons. He later went into the army for two years' national service. In exchange, his father agreed to pay off his gambling debts. Goldsmith was already a confirmed gambler, and had been ever since his prep school days at Millfield where he used to bet on horses with postal orders. Every endeavour was a game which could be won or lost. 'The trouble with the British,' he told David Frost, 'is that we have not been told which game we are playing.' Such a man, like his brother Teddy, was a welcome recruit to the John Aspinall gang of the early fifties. What is more, he was able to cash cheques at all his father's hotels. Once, when a cheque bounced, he stormed round to his bank with Aspinall and poured a bottle of ink over the bank manager's head, shouting 'I'll take my overdraft elsewhere'.

In 1953 Goldsmith found himself involved in a rather more serious game when he met and fell in love with Isabel, the sixteen-year-old daughter of Don Antenor Patino, a Bolivian

35

tin magnate with a fortune of about £75 million. The Patinos, who wanted their daughter to marry into European royalty, were violently opposed to the match, but the following year the young couple, pursued by the world's press and an army of private detectives, eloped to Scotland and were married at Kelso. Four months later, Isabel died in childbirth at Paris. Her mother then abducted the baby and Goldsmith fought and won a long battle in the French courts to keep custody of the child.

The whole experience steeled Goldsmith's nerve and sobered him up. He now tried his hand in business, partly perhaps to show Patino that he could beat him at his own game, and from this time forward there is no doubting Goldsmith's will to succeed. He had drive. He was ruthless, and capable of working extremely hard. All the same, his first ventures were failures. Laboratories Cassine sold cheap cortisone tablets, but *The Lancet* criticised the quality of the drugs and the company flopped. In England, Goldsmith had entered the pharmacy business in partnership with a young man named Selim Zilkha, later to become famous as the Mothercare king. But this too was a flop. Goldsmith was left owning a small slimming-food company.

It was not until 1962 that he had any real success. He now teamed up with an extremely wealthy man and a distant relative, the Baron Alexis de Gunzburg, heir to one of the biggest fortunes in France. They took over a tramway company in Algeria, now renamed Generale Occidentale, and expanded it into their master company. Two years later Cavenham was formed, based on Goldsmith's slimming-food company. He and de Gunzburg then embarked on a buying spree, and in the course of a few years Cavenham took over a series of firms making biscuits, snuff, jam and all manner of comestibles — even marzipan mice. The empire expanded. There were supermarkets in Europe and America, a stake in the Eiffel Tower, a manganese mine in Africa. Goldsmith built a complicated maze of businesses, banks and property companies. There were occasional setbacks, and in 1966 the Cavenham accounts were qualified by the auditors. Ten years later, however, all seemed set fair.

But was it? Despite the range of his activities and the size of the turnover, Goldsmith's reputation, especially in the City of London, did not seem as secure as it ought to be. Not surprisingly, with my limited knowledge of finance, I found it difficult to unravel the workings of his empire, but I was relieved to discover that even the experts had a similar problem. They talked of Goldsmith in the same breath as 'Tiny' Rowland and Jim Slater — people, that is, whose operations could not be said to be attractive from the investor's point of view because it was never clear what precisely they were up to. Commentators wrote of Goldsmith as a conjurer, or a Houdini, engaged in a series of feats or tricks — creating smokescreens, pulling off deals, or running rings round his opponents.

Now at the age of forty-three, Goldsmith was playing a new game. He was already the head of a huge business empire, but like many men of his age he felt dissatisfied, experiencing the same stirrings as Don Quixote, who, at the age of forty, was suddenly seized with the urge to put the world to rights.

> 'Now these dispositions being made, he would no longer defer putting his design into execution, being the more strongly excited thereto by the mischief he thought his delay occasioned in the world; such and so many were the grievances he proposed to redress, the wrongs he intended to rectify, the exorbitances to correct, the abuses to reform, and the debts to discharge.'

It is a common phenomenon for businessmen who have built up huge organisations to think that their skills and experience can be harnessed to the national purpose. If only, they think, decisions could be taken and implemented quickly without all the bureaucratic delay and compromising that goes on. Cecil King, former Chairman of IPC, publishers of the *Daily Mirror*, is perhaps the best-known recent example of a man who dreamed of a government consisting of top industrialists like himself and Lord Robens, brought in to sort things out. Now Goldsmith was bitten by the same bug. Soon his powerful Teutonic accents could be heard at meetings and lunches, laying down the law about what needed to be done. But his ambitions, like those of King, seemed to ignore the difficulty of by-passing the well-established democratic processes in Britain or of coming in over the heads of politicians who have been slowly working their way up the greasy pole for years and years. What will make them agree to defer to a group of entrepreneurs? For it is rare for businessmen to be prepared to go through the humdrum preliminaries of a political career — that long dreary round of meetings and speeches — or to countenance the possibility of electoral defeat and loss of office.

By natural inclination a man of the extreme right, Goldsmith first showed signs of political ambition during the Tory administration of 1970-74. He became a close friend of the then Prime Minister, Edward Heath, and helped to raise funds for him in 1974. But Heath lost the election and the following year he was ousted from the Tory leadership. Goldsmith quickly fell out of favour with Mrs Thatcher, Heath's successor, who did not appreciate the political notions of the Clermont Club. For the time being it looked as if Goldsmith's ambitions were thwarted.

Then, in the summer of 1975, a new opening appeared. Through his friend Jim Slater, Goldsmith had been introduced to David Frost. Frost's ill-fated Equity Enterprises was largely financed by Slater Walker money and Frost had conceived a fanatical devotion to Slater. There was a story of how, while talking to a friend at a party, Frost pointed to a solitary rose in a jug of water, and said with great feeling 'Jim is just as interested in how that rose withers and dies as in any of his business deals.' Frost knew the Prime Minister, Harold Wilson, and a great admirer of his was Wilson's powerful aide, Lady Falkender, formerly Marcia Williams, who had a particular penchant not only for show-business personalities but also for self-made millionaires. Frost combined the two roles. Frost himself, meanwhile, had taken a shine to Goldsmith and invited him to appear on his latest TV programme, *We British*. Better still, he was able to arrange an introduction to Wilson. Some time in July 1975, a dinner party took place at Frost's London house. The guests included Wilson, Falkender and Goldsmith. (Curiously, this dinner party was mentioned in the 'Grovel' column of *Private Eye*, though at the time no one attached any great significance to it.) Some weeks later, Frost took Goldsmith down to 10 Downing Street for the first of several meetings to discuss French economic planning methods. According to his press secretary, Joe Haines, Wilson was very impressed by Goldsmith's mastery of financial matters. There was also, at a later stage, a lunch at Number Ten attended by Goldsmith and Lord Ryder, then head of the National Enterprise Board. The discussion again revolved around French planning and what lessons Britain could learn from her Common Market partner.

In February 1976, the Paris correspondent of the *Evening Standard*, Sam White, wrote a long article on Goldsmith. White knows him very well, ever since he covered the Patino elopement, and freely admits that Goldsmith has given him some of his best stories in the past. He now wrote a piece, plainly inspired by Goldsmith himself, in which was spelled out this food tycoon's desire for pastures new in the shape of a political career. But, it seemed, Goldsmith was worried by his curious marital arrangements. Would his two families be held against him?

A far more serious setback to Goldsmith's budding political career came a few weeks later, on 16 March, when his new found friend and potential patron, Harold Wilson, announced his resignation. The news took everyone, apart from a few insiders, completely by surprise, so much so that many people can, as with President Kennedy's assassination, vividly remember the circumstances in which they heard the news. This reaction was in itself rather surprising, as Wilson had in fact been considering retirement for well over a year, and possibly even longer. When he became Prime Minister for the second time around in March 1974, it was plain that he relished the job less keenly than before. The trappings of power, the visits to Buckingham Palace, everything he most enjoyed about being Prime Minister, were no longer a novelty to him. His retirement was therefore a perfectly logical development.

All the same, the news when it came was to most people a shock. Reaction was mixed. First there was alarm, apparent in tumbling share prices, for despite his unpopularity the feeling was widespread that Wilson, who had been Labour leader for so long, alone had the ability to keep the government and the country together at a time of economic difficulty. At the same time there was a last wave of hostility towards him, on the grounds that he appeared to be getting out while the going was good. Thirdly, there were rumours. Wilson's departure, it was said, was due to some hidden scandal that would soon break.

However, the weeks passed. No terrible crisis ensued, no scandal emerged, and as the Labour Party set about electing a new leader in a relatively dignified and orderly way, the fears and the rumours receded in people's minds. Perhaps, all things considered, Wilson had done the right thing by resigning. An election was not due for another two years, and in the meantime he had given his successor, who turned out to be James Callaghan, a chance to establish himself as a new Prime Minister with a new style of government. Wilson, it seemed, might have acted in a statesmanlike manner after all.

Then an episode occurred which, at a stroke, reversed the goodwill which Wilson was recovering and cast a shadow not just on his resignation but, it seemed, on his whole premiership. The first indication of the storm that was to break came on 2 May 1976 when the *Sunday Times* revealed exclusively that Wilson's resignation Honours List had run into difficulties.

Since the scandal over Lloyd George's sale of honours, the Maundy Gregory affair, a Political Honours Scrutiny Committee has existed to vet all political honours lists. It consists of three elder statesmen, one for each of the three main political parties. In 1976, the year of Wilson's resignation, the Committee consisted of Lord Crathorne (Conservative), the Minister who resigned over the Crichel Down affair, even though he was not directly responsible, Baroness Summerskill (Labour), and Lord Rea (Liberal).

Wilson's list, according to the *Sunday Times* report, had been drawn up with the assistance of his political and personal office, headed by Lady Falkender. Wilson himself, however, had deleted several names, including that of David Frost who at the time was engaged in arranging a lucrative TV contract with Wilson. 'In the circumstances,' the *Sunday Times* said, 'he felt it would not be appropriate for him to put Mr Frost forward.'

But the main point of the story was that the Scutiny Committee had now objected to three life peers on the Wilson list.

'One of the names is that of a City financier, another is a financier and impresario, and the third is a minor businessman.'

The *Sunday Times*, it seemed, knew the identities of these men but did not like to reveal them. However, it did not need much investigation on my part among friends on the paper to discover that the City financier was Goldsmith. (The financier and impresario was a certain Jarvis Astaire — whose activities in the boxing world were regularly featured in *Private Eye* — and the minor businessman was Wilson's friend, the Gannex mackintosh manufacturer, Sir Joseph Kagan.)

A further mystery was the identity of the person, presumably a senior figure, who had leaked the story to the newspaper. Whoever he was, he plainly was not satisfied with the *Sunday Times*'s treatment of its scoop. A little over two weeks later, on 19 May, the front page of the *Daily Express* bore the extraordinary headline, 'It's LORD GOLDSMITH !' The paper stated categorically that Goldsmith had accepted the offer of a peerage.

41

This was a truly bizarre development. For what had Goldsmith done to deserve such an honour? Apart from his few recent meetings with Wilson, he had always been a Tory supporter, and his companies had donated money to the Tory party.

By this stage, however, *Private Eye* had no time left to pursue such speculations, for our legal battle had just entered a strange new phase.

The Attempt to Settle

From the beginning everyone had been naturally puzzled as to the motives behind Goldsmith's massive legal bombardment of *Private Eye*. A number of explanations were put forward.

Firstly there was his well-documented aversion to unfavourable publicity of any kind, for example, the James Fox article. If Goldsmith reacted to that piece by ostracising one of his best friends, who subsequently committed suicide, what was odd about him adopting a similarly exaggerated attitude to *Private Eye*?

Nor, after all, was this the first occasion on which he had issued writs. The *Observer* had been recently sued following a feature on the Cavenham-owned Marmite. In 1975 Goldsmith sued *The Economist* when he considered himself libelled by an article about City whizz-kids. Goldsmith's reaction to any intrusion into his private life was even more extreme. Once, for example, at a party in Gstaad given by Roman Polanski, the notorious film director, Goldsmith had snatched a camera from a girl photographing the guests and smashed it to pieces. This aversion to publicity stemmed perhaps from the Patino episode, when Goldsmith and Isabel had been ruthlessly pursued by hordes of journalists over Scotland.

In 1971, at the time of Goldsmith's takeover of Bovril, there occurred a more serious intrusion into his affairs when Richard Milner, a financial journalist on the *Sunday Times Business News*, began an investigation into the complicated structure of Cavenham and its offshoots. Milner arrived for an interview at Goldsmith's house in Chester Terrace. But at an early stage Goldsmith decided that the *Sunday Times* man was an enemy.

Milner was more than a little surprised when Goldsmith, accompanied by Eric Levine, later accused him before the *Business News* Editor of arriving at his house drunk, damaging his accoutrements, being 'part of a vast and incredibly sinister conspiracy against him', becoming drunker and kicking his dog. (The oddest thing, as Sherlock Holmes might have remarked, was that there was no dog.)

Milner's prime source was an ex-employee of Nestlé, Geoffrey Pinder. This poor man found himself subjected to even stranger treatment. Goldsmith had succeeded in identifying him with the help of private detectives, who later, so Pinder claimed, had harassed him. His phone would ring in the middle of the night, strangers knocked at his door, his car was followed, and in the end he retired to Switzerland suffering from an obsession with Goldsmith.

To us at *Private Eye*, all this suggested a man who was, to put it mildly, extremely sensitive to all forms of criticism, liable to fly off the handle at any time. But if this was the case, why had there been such a long delay following the publication of the Elwes article and the issuing of the writs? After all, two further issues of the *Eye*, both containing attacks on Goldsmith, had been published before he sued.

It was the fact that the second of the two articles referred to his solicitor, Eric Levine, which seemed to point to another explanation of the barrage of writs. Was it not possible that *Private Eye*, by mentioning Levine, had accidentally stumbled on some potential source of embarrassment, or worse, to Goldsmith, and that he had issued all the writs in a desperate attempt to prevent any further revelations?

In our new mood of seriousness following the Wien judgement, which had turned the case into one of Criminal Libel, we decided that Patrick Marnham and myself would go back over the Lucan story and see if there was anything to be salvaged for our defence. At the same time, an old friend, Andrew Osmond, the original backer of *Private Eye*, offered his services to gather general information about Goldsmith, while Michael Gillard volunteered to pursue the Levine story.

We knew little about Levine at this stage apart from what had been written in the *Eye* article. But gradually more information emerged. Eric Anthony Levine was the son of a Sunderland draper. He was born in 1936. He read law at London University and was taken on by the solicitors Paisner & Co, a firm with a number of wealthy City clients and businessmen, including Sir Isaac Wolfson and also the late Sir Allen Lane, founder of Penguin Books. Levine specialised in company law, and throughout his career had been as much a businessman as a lawyer. It was while at Paisner's that he formed his association with a client of the firm, T. Dan Smith, and became Chairman of Vinleigh Ltd, part of Smith's 'public relations' empire. Smith, we learned later, had an exceptionally high regard for Levine's business acumen. In 1968 the two men became directors of Tyne Tees Television. Levine left Paisner's the following year in circumstances that had given rise to rumours about misconduct. After a short period working as a consultant for Sir Charles Forte, he formed his own firm of solicitors and was taken up by Goldsmith who had also been for a short time a Paisner client. Levine became a director of the Goldsmith-financed property company, Argyle Securities, and acquired a sumptuous office building next door to the Clermont Club, which he decorated with antique furnishings, chandeliers and sprays of flowers. Everything suggested that now, thanks to his connection with Goldsmith, Levine was successful and rich.

It was because of the link with Sir Charles Forte that Gillard, unbeknownst to me, approached his old friend John Addey, whose firm, John Addey & Associates, handled public relations for Trust House Forte.

I myself had first met Addey in 1970 when I was invited by George Hutchinson to address a Fleet Street gathering of the Whitefriars Club, the members of which are mostly journalists. During question time there were a number of hostile remarks about *Private Eye* from the floor, whereupon a young man of rather boyish appearance sitting near the platform rose to his feet and defended the *Eye* in the most enthusiastic terms as a vital institution of British life. After the meeting I asked to be introduced to my champion. It was John Addey, a highly successful public relations consultant whose clients included a number of big firms like Tesco and Trust House Forte. Addey was also an expert on City takeovers, in which he frequently acted as advisor to one of the two parties. Some days after the Whitefriars meeting he invited me to lunch with some City journalists at his luxurious flat in the Albany. Addey, a vivacious and attentive host, seemed to be a fund of political and financial gossip, an excellent source for *Private Eye*. Thereafter he became a regular attender at our Wednesday lunches in The Coach and Horses. At the same time, though I was not aware of it, he was giving stories to Michael Gillard, then on the *Daily Express*. There were a number of occasions, too, on which Gillard was able to assist Addey by supplying him with information.

A few days after the Criminal Libel hearing, Gillard rang Addey on the off-chance that, because of his connection with Forte, he might know something about Levine. Like most friends of *Private Eye* at the time, Addey had been outraged by the Wien verdict and was anxious to help in any way possible. When, therefore, Gillard mentioned the rumours of misconduct while Levine was working at Paisner's, Addey volunteered at once: 'Why don't I ring Paisner? He's an old mate.'

This was a great stroke of luck and, true to his word, Addey immediately contacted Leslie Paisner. For the lawyer's benefit he concocted a story about an American client of his who was thinking of suing Levine. Rather to his surprise, Paisner agreed to see him.

Addey called on Paisner on 20 April 1976 and the two men had a long talk. During the course of it Paisner described how he had taken on Levine fresh from law school in 1961 and how, on three separate occasions subsequently, Levine had been guilty of professional misconduct.

Addey had arranged to have dinner with Gillard the following day in order to report back to him. Meanwhile, that same day, by a pure coincidence, Addey himself was due to attend the *Private Eye* lunch traditionally held in a grubby upstairs room at The Coach and Horses in Greek Street.

These lunches, held every alternate Wednesday, have been going on for several years now. About twelve people attend, four of them from *Private Eye* — myself, Patrick Marnham, Martin Tomkinson and Auberon Waugh. The others are guests, mostly journalists, who are expected to some extent to 'sing for their supper' by providing *Private Eye* with information.

As often happened, Addey rang me shortly beforehand and asked if he could bring a friend with him — in this case a journalist on the *Daily Telegraph* who knew details of Levine's activities in the property field. There were a number of other journalists present, among them Brian McConnell of the *News of the World*. Another guest was Brian Walden, then Labour MP for Birmingham Ladywood.

Addey arrived in a state of almost uncontrollable excitement. He drew me at once to one side to break the news about Levine. He could not talk about it in detail at the lunch, he said, but he was seeing Gillard that evening and would give him chapter and verse. One remark of Paisner's that he quoted stuck in my mind, and I made a note of it at the time: 'A man like Goldsmith needs a lawyer like Levine.' During the lunch itself, Addey sat opposite me and was his normal voluble self, speaking freely to all and sundry about Goldsmith and Levine. He was, I remember, full of scurrilous stories about Jeremy Thorpe, then coming under fire on account of the Norman Scott affair.

That was altogether a very strange day. After the lunch I returned to *Private Eye* and was more than alarmed to find Michael Gillard slumped over a desk, apparently suffering from the appalling effects of food poisoning. He seemed so ill that I thought he might be incapable of keeping his vital appointment with Addey that evening. A taxi had already been ordered to take him home. So when I left at about six, I asked Martin Tomkinson, then nobly playing the part of male nurse, to go and see Addey himself if Gillard was not well enough to get to the Albany.

In fact, as I learned the following day, Gillard made a remarkable and complete recovery, although he was an hour or two late for his dinner engagement. He arrived at the Albany at about ten, to find Addey on the steps, waving and smiling. They walked on to Burke's in Bond Street, where Addey had booked a table at the back of the restaurant. Over the meal Addey repeated to Gillard everything Paisner had told him about Levine, giving him details for the three occasions on which, so Paisner claimed, Levine had acted improperly. Gillard then asked Addey if he had found out anything about Levine's brief period working for Sir Charles Forte. No, Addey said, he had been unable to contact Forte himself but would try to speak to another friend of his in the organisation.

During their ensuing conversation Gillard referred, as he had done in his previous telephone call, to the fact that *Private Eye* had been sent, about eighteen months previously, an anonymous communication about the state of Addey's business. Written in the style of a 'Colour Section' item, the letter, which would seem to have been sent by a disgruntled employee or ex-employee, listed a number of things that were wrong in Addey's firm. (*Private Eye* is constantly in receipt of such anonymous material.) At the time I had passed it to Marnham, who in turn had passed it on to Gillard, who, being a compulsive hoarder of documents, had kept it, intending to give it to Addey at the first opportunity. But Gillard and Addey had not in fact met since that time. I myself had long forgotten the letter's existence. But later it was to assume great significance.

Over dinner, Gillard, who had intended, prior to his attack of food poisoning, to bring the letter with him tried to recall its contents. There had been some mention of protective notices being issued to some members of Addey's staff, also of a party costing £2,000 — Gillard remembered this because he had been one of the guests — and lastly of the fact that Addey had been

48

unable to keep on his chauffeur. Addey said it all sounded like a true account of things at the time, though, happily, the situation was now more healthy. They agreed that it must have been sent by one of Addey's staff, and Addey joked that the letter was so accurate he must have written it himself. The two men left the restaurant at about midnight and walked back to the Albany, down Bond Street. They parted on excellent terms, and Gillard said he would send on to Addey the anonymous letter so that he could see for himself what had been written.

Gillard reported back to me the following day. We decided that, because of the seriousness of the Paisner allegations, it was not enough to rely on Addey's evidence. Someone should go and see Paisner and hear the story from his own lips. Patrick Marnham volunteered.

Our intention at this stage was, in so far as we thought about it at all, to muster as strong a defence in the Levine libel action and thus be in a better position if it came to any bargaining with Goldsmith. Any material to the discredit of Levine was obviously very helpful in this way. A secondary possibility was a further piece in *Private Eye* about Levine.

A day or two later Marnham rang Paisner, who seemed to be expecting the call. 'Do you know why I am ringing?' Marnham asked. 'Yes,' Paisner replied, 'E.L.' They arranged to meet on the morning of Wednesday, 5 May. In view of Paisner's position, Marnham decided to wear a tie.

Leslie Lazarus Paisner, sixty-eight, was the senior partner of Paisner & Co, a highly successful solicitor working mainly for big businessmen. Marnham found a small, grey-haired man, cordial and relaxed, who began by saying that in normal circumstances he would not dream of talking to *Private Eye*. But the fact that we were under threat of criminal proceedings, and that there was a possibility of a prison sentence, made things different. He went on to talk about Eric Levine.

Levine, he said, had come to his firm in 1961 as an articled clerk. Paisner had given him a job on the recommendation of a friend who, as Professor of Law, had taught Levine at London

49

University. He had turned out to be a very promising pupil and in due course became Paisner's protégé. But then the day came when some of the partners in the firm made allegations against Levine, urging Paisner to dismiss him. Paisner, reluctant to believe anything to the discredit of his favourite, refused; Levine would learn his lesson, he insisted. But then a second incident occurred. Again Paisner gave Levine the benefit of the doubt. Only when it happened a third time did Paisner part company with Levine. They had not met or spoken since.

Marnham then asked Paisner why, in view of all that had happened, he had not reported Levine to the disciplinary committee of the Law Society. Paisner replied that he had, above all, wanted to protect the good name of his firm.

As to Goldsmith, he had been a client of Paisner's in his early days, but was the only major one subsequently to defect to Levine.

Paisner then went on to talk about *Private Eye*. He was evidently concerned about the growth of corruption in London, which, he said, was frightening. He strongly approved of *Private Eye*'s role in exposing men like Levine and said he would ask his partners if they could help the magazine in any other way. But he especially insisted that we should make our own independent enquiries and should not rely on his evidence alone. He mentioned the names of one or two former clients of his firm whom he thought might prove helpful, and concluded by saying he would certainly consider another meeting with Marnham.

At this point in the story Goldsmith had not set the Criminal Libel ball rolling. He was still, as we put it in *Private Eye*, 'fingering with some trepidation the antique blunderbuss which Mr Justice Wien in a fit of untypical exuberance has put in his hands.' The next stage in the legal proceedings was for Goldsmith to 'lay information' at Bow Street which would result in the police issuing a summons against me, and obviously he could make use of this situation as one in which to bargain for a settlement.

50

Meanwhile, we, too, had been making preparations. I had already had one meeting to discuss the Criminal Libel case with our new QC, James Comyn. He was a small, stooping, bespectacled Irishman, rather shabbily dressed, his trousers frayed, his cuffs white with the ash of Sweet Aftons which he chain-smoked. His room in Queen Elizabeth Building with its high windows looking out on to the Embankment was in a state of Dickensian chaos. Bundles of briefs and law books lay piled all over the floor. There was what looked like a bottle of eggnog under a table in the corner. 'Well,' he said, when we were all seated, 'we seem to be in check. But is it checkmate?'

Now, on Thursday 6 May, the day after Marnham's meeting with Paisner, another meeting with Comyn had been arranged to discuss the possibility of reaching an out-of-court settlement with Goldsmith. Comyn who at the time appreciated better, I think, than I did the weakness of our position in the Criminal Libel case, counselled strongly in favour of a settlement. He thought we would probably lose the criminal action and, though he did not think that a judge would send me to prison, it was not out of the question. A fine of about £20,000 was, he thought, the most likely outcome.

Hawser, Goldsmith's QC, had by this time indicated that his client was prepared to settle for the following terms — Comyn called them 'Luneberg Heath terms' — which would have to be agreed by that weekend:

(i) Damages of £15 — £20,000;
(ii) An apology in open court, to be published in *Private Eye* and two other papers;
(iii) An agreement by *Private Eye* not to mention either Goldsmith or Levine for five years and thereafter to submit any material about either of them forty-eight hours before publication (thus giving them the opportunity to go to court and seek an injunction);
(v) Disclosure of the names of the authors of the offending articles, who, provided they apologised, would be

given immunity from further litigation.

(From various clues, now and later, it emerged that Goldsmith was convinced that Nigel Dempster had written the Elwes article and that he was determined to get some kind of confession from him. In this assumption Goldsmith was, of course, wrong. Dempster had supplied a draft on Elwes, but Marnham had written the finished article.)

On this last point, Hawser had quoted Goldsmith as saying that he was determined to know the identity of the authors. 'Unless he gets the names,' Hawser had told Comyn, 'he will move heaven and earth to identify them and he will hound them.' Hawser himself was, it seemed, equally insistent that Levine should be protected by the agreement. 'A different timbre comes into his voice when he mentions the Levine point,' Comyn said, and from this we deduced that Goldsmith had got wind of our investigations into Levine.

Yet it was the Levine clause which, more than any other, stuck in my gullet. Why should we give Eric Levine any guarantees when he had not issued a writ, nor even threatened to do so? Alternatively, looking at it from Goldsmith's point of view, why, if he felt that his lawyer was vulnerable, did he not simply jettison him and hire another? This was to become one of the most intriguing and, in the end, unanswered questions in the story.

Over that weekend, in a series of rather frantic phone calls, the negotiations went on. Goldsmith withdrew his demand for damages, he withdrew the five-year ban on a mention of his name. But he still wanted the forty-eight hour vetting procedure for himself and Levine and the names of the authors. I did not like the vetting idea but offered instead that we 'would agree before publishing any information to give the opportunity to reply and to print the substance of their reply.' Gillard, who had some experience of these matters, insisted on the proviso that 'they in turn would agree to be available' in such a situation.

The weekend deadline expired. Levine named twelve o'clock on Monday as a new deadline. But that too went by. In the end, exasperated by the delay, I turned the tables and decided to give the other side a deadline. We would offer an apology, costs, and a guarantee to check information in advance, and they had until four o'clock that afternoon to accept. Not surprisingly, perhaps, my deadline went by without their agreement.

The settlement had broken down, and next day Goldsmith laid information at Bow Street.

Afterwards Goldsmith and Hawser reiterated at every opportunity that I had broken off negotiations because I was not prepared to agree never to attack Levine, at least without giving him warning in advance. In fact, though stumbling blocks are cited as the cause of breakdown in negotiations, it is more often the case that one party creates a stumbling block because it does not really want to settle. Thinking about it, the more reluctant I became to do any deal with Goldsmith whatsoever. Perhaps it was something to do with his bullying talk about 'hounding' us, Elwes-style, or his arrogant assumption that he could control what *Private Eye* said about him. At any rate, when the negotiations finally broke down, my feeling was one of apprehension but also of relief.

I suppose, if I am to be honest, another reason was that in spite of all the stress, part of me was enjoying the excitement of the case and did not want it to end at this point. A few weeks later I met Goldsmith's brother, Teddy, at a party. 'You should be grateful to my brother, Mr Ingrams, ' he said with a rather wild grin. 'He has made your life more interesting.

It was perfectly true.

Volte Face

On the afternoon of 17 May, a week after the settlement talks broke down and the same day on which a sheepish policeman ambled round to *Private Eye* with a summons, Michael Gillard's secretary at Granada Television took a phone call from a man in an extreme state of agitation. He refused to give his name. 'I'm a friend,' he said. 'He will know who it is. Tell him that one of his main stories has collapsed disastrously. It will be murder for him tomorrow. It was very nasty.'

Gillard did not get this message until later that day. But the same afternoon I myself received news from our solicitor, Geoffrey Bindman, that Goldsmith was applying for an *ex parte* injunction against not only *Private Eye* but Patrick Marnham, Michael Gillard, Nigel Dempster, Auberon Waugh and Richard West as well, to stop any of us writing about himself or Eric Levine pending the hearing of the libel actions.

This seemed an inexplicable thing to do, and on my way home on the train that night I tried to work out what Goldsmith's motives might be. Why drag in Dempster and Waugh? Dempster had recently annoyed him, I knew, by writing an unflattering paragraph about one of his odd-job men, Peter West, a penniless Clermont Club gambler who — so Dempster alleged — was being dunned for £500 by a businessman. A letter of complaint from Goldsmith to the *Daily Mail* had spoken of 'a further step in a conspiracy to harass Mr Goldsmith's friends and acquaintances because of their relationship with him.' This talk of a conspiracy was something new, and I thought it might explain his application for an injunction. He was taking extra measures, perhaps, against what he perceived as an extra threat.

The hearing being *ex parte* (or 'on one side only'), there was nothing we could do except go along to the Law Courts next day and hear what they had to say. All the same, I rang Geoffrey Bindman that evening at his home to find out if he knew what was happening. 'If you hang on,' he said, 'Levine's have just delivered a whole lot of papers here and I can tell you.'

I waited. Then Bindman came back on the line, sounding surprised. 'There's an affidavit from someone called John Addey,' he said, 'and one from Leslie Paisner.' He started to read them out. As he went on, his voice began to falter. 'I can't believe it,' he said. 'It's incredible.'

The following morning, Gillard and I met Geoffrey Bindman and Desmond Browne, our junior counsel, at the law Courts. Goldsmith, who now for the first time appeared in the flesh — was refused an *ex parte* injunction and the judge ordered a hearing at which both sides could present their case. *Private Eye* agreed not to mention Goldsmith or Levine until the hearing which was expected to be in a few days' time.

In the meantime, we had a chance to study in detail the two affidavits which had stupefied Bindman on the phone. This was Paisner's, sworn and signed at his home two days earlier, on Sunday, 16 May:

> 'After Eric Levine left Paisner & Co, the firm of which I am senior partner, in October 1969, I have deliberately on a number of occasions seriously defamed him. [Paisner then listed the incidents he had described to Addey and Marnham.] I hereby unequivocally acknowledge that all these statements and allegations were lies and without any foundation whatsoever. They were part of a vicious vendetta perpetrated by me on Eric Levine. I withdraw each and every one of them unreservedly. I made these outrageous allegation against Eric Levine because his departure from the firm, particularly to join

Charles Forte, who was one of my personal friends and clients, was a major blow to me. Also, my relationship with Eric Levine had been a close one. His departure turned my feelings to hatred. Despite my attacks against Eric Levine, he prospered. The success of his firm embittered me the more, particularly when I learnt that the successful Jimmy Goldsmith had become his client. In his early days he (Goldsmith) had been a client of my firm.

When John Addey came to see me on 20 April....I saw this as an opportunity . . . . to ensure that Eric Levine would be ruined. I therefore told Addey a pack of lies about him and that I regretted the day I ever met him. John Addey yesterday confessed to me that all he told me was a pack of lies fabricated to get information from me about Eric Levine for *Private Eye* who were blackmailing him (Addey) and who were embarked on a campaign of vilification against Eric Levine.

Then, when Patrick Marnham called me on the 5th May to ask what I knew about Eric Levine, I saw yet another opportunity to bring about Eric Levine's downfall without being seen to be involved myself. I therefore repeated to *Private Eye* what I had told Addey and other seriously damaging statements.

All that I told John Addey and Patrick Marnham of *Private Eye* was a complete pack of lies from beginning to end and without any truth or foundation. I have withdrawn all these statements and allegations.

I am deeply ashamed of my conduct. Only now do I fully understand how vindictive it has been and what harm and damage I have caused Eric Levine. I now wish to put an end to the campaign I mounted against Eric Levine and ensure that he suffers no further damage as a result of the lies I have told about him.'

So much for Paisner's statement. John Addey's had been sworn two days previously, on Friday, 14 May, at Goldsmith's offices in Leadenhall Street. It read as follows:

'I was telephoned by Michael Gillard on 13th April, and was asked if I would meet him for dinner. We arranged to meet on 21st April. In the meantime, he wanted to talk on the telephone. We had not, according to him, met for two years or so, although I thought it had been about eighteen months. He began, after friendly preliminaries, to talk about harmful information he had received about my firm and me personally — the former from, he suggested, a previous employee, and the latter about a homosexual liaison.

He thought I should know the latter verbally, and that he would in any event return the former — which he quoted, in detailed form, 'from memory'. It was vindictive and biased, but based on some fact, and also included a personal and homosexual implication.

He then said he was pursuing an enquiry into a lawyer, Eric Levine . . . . He thought I should help, since THF (Trust House Forte) were clients, and Paisner he knew I knew. The plain implication was the threat that, if I did not help, *Private Eye* would print damaging things about my firm and me personally . . . . I realised it was a serious matter, but knew that I was not prepared to involve Sir Charles Forte in any way, nor could I afford, if it were possible, to have PE [*sic*] print the material about me. I did not know whether the material was true or false, though I realised that Jimmy Goldsmith was suing *Private Eye*, and a lateral attack, while no defence, offered a potential trading position.

On the Tuesday morning, 20th April, Gillard telephoned again and said he wanted the information as soon as possible. I called Paisner straight afterwards and asked if Levine was straight or not. He sounded shaken, said he could not discuss it on the telephone, and asked me to come round at 1.00. I could not, as I was lunching

57

in Regent's Park with my daughter's mother, but arranged to see him at 12.45, which I did.

I asked him to tell me his experience of Eric Levine and he asked me why. I told him an American bank was involved, and there was a client of theirs who had been involved in a business deal with Levine. Could she deal and trust him [*sic*]? He told me in strictest confidence and to tell no one. He said that Eric Levine had been a partner and he had taken him on as an articled clerk. He was brilliant, should have got a First, but had liked the bright lights too much.

[After mentioning the details of Paisner's allegations, Addey went on to give an account of his own questions about Levine.] Why, I asked, did he now act for Goldsmith if he had such a history? Paisner said, 'Some people need to have a lawyer like that.' Why, then, had Sir Charles, whom I believed wholeheartedly to be absolutely correct, taken him on? He said he had advised Charles Forte not to do so, but had been told by Forte 'Don't tell me whom I take on,' and there had been a consequent rift in the relationship. He ended by telling me this was on a no-tell basis and I agreed, and left. I lunched the following day at *Private Eye*. They had asked me two months or so before. At lunch, Eric Levine's name was not mentioned, though Richard Ingrams was visibly anxious about his battle with Jimmy Goldsmith and said *Private Eye* had been wrong in fact though right in spirit.

As we left, I said to Ingrams: 'I hope you'll not print anything about me', and he said: 'Too much on my plate to have another case.'

That same evening, 21st April, [Addey's statement went on] I was to dine with Gillard. I had considered my position and believed that, whatever the outcome for me, I was smallish fry in a Criminal Libel case, and I could not get involved in passing information on. My meeting with Paisner had been on terms which debarred discussion with anyone. I booked a table at Burke's at 10:30.

He covered the ground he had covered already . . . I told him I had seen Paisner, but had not been able to discuss the questions he had asked with him, and Paisner would not talk. Nor could I talk to Forte. He asked me again to do so, and went into detail on a press release from one of my ex-staff, a copy of which he thought I ought to see, and which he would send to me.

He said he was determined to discover the truth about Levine . . . . and would print the story, even though it would mean emigrating. That also I took as a threat.

[Addey then described how Gillard had sent him a copy of the so-called 'press release' with a note asking if he had seen Forte.] I took that also as a *quid-pro-quo* threat [he went on] that they would not print anything against me if I helped them with information on Levine, but I had already decided that I would neither report the Paisner conversation to anyone not would ever raise the matter — or Eric Levine's name — with Charles Forte or any of his colleagues, which I haven't, preferring to take the risk of a *Private Eye* piece on me.'

John Addey's statement ended there, and in view of his previously co-operative attitude it astonished us at *Private Eye* no less than it had our solicitor, Geoffrey Bindman.

Accordingly, after the hearing on 18 May in which Goldsmith's application for an injunction was rejected, I rang Addey several times. But on each occasion I was told that he was out. I left messages asking him to ring me.

Then the following day, the day on which the *Daily Express* carried its dramatic forecast of the Goldsmith peerage, I got a message from Addey to come round to the Albany at 12.45 p.m. He had a hunted look and was in a very agitated state. In spite of my contempt for what he had done, I could not help feeling sorry for him. I said I was sure he had made a dreadful mistake in going over to the other side, that his business would in the end be ruined, because once the story got out — as it was bound to do — journalists would refuse to talk to him. Addey maintained that he had had very little choice. Paisner, who he had seen over the weekend and who was apparently in a state of collapse, had retracted, and he, Addey, (who affected to accept Paisner's second statement at face value), had no alternative but to follow suit. Goldsmith and Levine, he claimed, had threatened him with a Criminal Libel action. 'I never realised they were so powerful', he said. I repeated that he had made a disastrous mistake and that it would ruin him. He said that, whatever happened, he thought his business was ruined. What should he do? I said the least he could do was to talk to Gillard. He agreed, to my surprise, to do this, and I said I would ring him and fix a time. As I left, he said: 'This conversation never took place, OK?' I agreed. At no point did I discuss his blackmail allegation.

Gillard was in fact unwilling to speak to Addey and so another meeting never took place. In view of what happened later, this was probably just as well. Addey and I have not spoken since.

At this point the reader may be no less confused than we ourselves were at this time. So let me recap the situation as it then stood. Both Leslie Paisner and John Addey, two men whom we believed to be firmly on our side in the investigation of Eric Levine, Goldsmith's private lawyer, had suddenly and dramatically swapped horses, producing statements in support of Goldsmith's requested injunction against *Private Eye* and other journalists said to be in a 'conspiracy' against him.

How had it happened?

With the help of a number of other affidavits, including two from Goldsmith himself, it was possible to reconstruct a rough sequence of events since the end of April.

On 28 April, a week after Addey had attended the *Private Eye* lunch and later had dinner with Gillard, Goldsmith had been told by his stockbroker, Sandy Gilmour, a partner in the firm of Joseph Sebag and a friend of Addey's, that *Private Eye* was preparing an attack on Eric Levine. Goldsmith had inferred that Gilmour's source must be Addey. Furthermore, it transpired that, at the time of the abortive settlement negotiations I have already described, Levine himself had been told privately by Geoffrey Bindman that our enquiries were centred on Levine's career at Paisner & Co.

Goldsmith had then questioned Levine, who insisted that Goldsmith himself should talk to Paisner. Accordingly, on 13 May, two days after the settlement broke down, Paisner had visited Goldsmith at his offices in Leadenhall Street and then repeated his story — how Addey had approached him with the story of the American client who was thinking of suing Levine, how he had seen Addey and what he had told Addey and later Marnham. Levine himself had then been summoned by Goldsmith and denied it all.

On the same afternoon that this confrontation occurred, Goldsmith had also asked his fellow director Roland Franklin, to bring Addey to his office. Addey had then gone round and repeated to Goldsmith what Paisner had told him about Levine.

At this point, therefore, Goldsmith had heard from two sources, Paisner and Addey, the same story about Levine's career at Paisner's.

Yet now, for no apparent reason, both men had changed their stories.

So exactly when, and why, had this change of heart occurred?

That question cannot be answered precisely. But again, working from the statements produced in support of Goldsmith's injunction, a rough scenario can be sketched.

On the evening after his summons by Goldsmith, Addey had rung Roland Franklin and admitted that his story of the American client — i.e. the story he had used to prompt Paisner into talking — had been untrue. Franklin had then 'invited' Addey to lunch the following day at Leadenhall Street. 'He was reluctant to explain the reasons for what he had done,' Franklin

61

wrote in his own statement, 'but finally said that they were related to the fact that he had had a homosexual relationship with somebody and was being blackmailed on that account.' Franklin then pointed out to Addey that he had seriously slandered Levine in his story of the fictitious American and, apparently, arranged for Eric Levine himself to call in after lunch.

At the appointed hour Levine had arrived, and he and Addey were left alone in Franklin's office.

After ten minutes of so, Levine emerged and told Franklin he could come back in. Addey then repeated what he had just told Levine — i.e. that he was being blackmailed by Gillard. Levine asked him if he would be prepared to swear a statement to this effect, and Addey agreed. Would he like a solicitor to be present? No, Addey said, he was happy to do it on his own. He then wrote his story out by hand and the draft was typed and signed and witnessed by a Commissioner for Oaths.

'He seemed much relieved', Franklin recorded, 'to have got the matter off his chest.'

Addey then, apparently, dictated two letters which were typed out on the Goldsmith typewriter. One was an apology to Eric Levine in which he admitted that he was 'deeply ashamed' of having slandered him by telling Paisner 'a pack of lies' about Levine and the American client.

'I beg your forgiveness', the letter ended strangely.

The second letter was to Paisner. This too spoke of 'a pack of lies', and ended, also in the style of the confessional: 'I am deeply ashamed of my conduct.'

According to a second statement by Addey which was dictated by Goldsmith in person a few days later, Paisner himself was informed that same afternoon, either by Gold-smith or Levine, of Addey's confession. He too was urged to sign a statement, but after conferring with his two sons — both partners in the firm — he refused. By the following morning (Saturday, 15 May), however, his attitude had for some reason changed. He rang Addey early in a state of agitation and the two arranged to meet at Paisner's Marylebone flat that afternoon. In response apparently to Addey's urging, Paisner then rang Levine and agreed to sign a statement. He did so the next day at his flat, though curiously the affidavit was typed on Levine's office typewriter.

To my own mind, Addey's statement, not least in its grammatical construction, bore all the marks of haste and almost of panic, though he later told a friend of mine that he and Franklin had consumed a whole bottle of brandy at their lunch. There were also scribbled alterations and deletions which suggested that, as he wrote, with Franklin and Levine perhaps looking over his shoulder, anomalies occurred to him which needed correction.

At the end of the first paragraph, for example, where he had written 'harmful information .... about a homosexual liaison', he went on to write, but on second thoughts crossed out, the words: ' .... with a banker who had been with a client of my firm'. (These words became legible, as so often happens, after the document had been photocopied several times.)

As for the anonymous note sent to *Private Eye*, he described it as a 'press release', yet Addey, who issued them all the time, knew perfectly well what a press release was and that the note was nothing like one.

These, and others like them, were minor discrepancies suggesting a man writing in great haste. But the statement was illogical in more basic ways. Addey wrote for example, quite truthfully, that he had seen Paisner, who had passed on the details of Levine's misconduct. He then asserted that he *decided not to pass the information on to Gillard*. And yet, on learning this, Gillard, the supposed blackmailer, not only failed to carry out his threat by exposing Addey, he apparently sat through a long dinner and even sent Addey the incriminating letter that he was allegedly using to threaten him with.

In his statement Addey ignored, too, the fact that a few hours before his evening meeting with Gillard he had been at the *Private Eye* lunch and had spoken quite freely to me, although

63

not in detail, of his meeting with Paisner, quoting for example, Paisner's remark that: 'A man like Goldsmith needs a lawyer like Levine.' At that lunch he had also regaled the company with anti-Goldsmith stories — behaviour which was in no way consistent either with a man who was being blackmailed or who had decided that his lips must remain sealed on the subject of Levine.

Ironically, too, Addey as good as admitted in his statement to being a homosexual, the very charge that we had supposedly threatened him with. This fact was now bound to be published, and it did not take us long to discover that it was true. But it was something of which Gillard and myself had both been completely unaware. I had seen nothing whatever at his Albany flat to suggest a homosexual menage, and neither had Gillard, who had often dined there. Plainly, in heterosexual company, Addey concealed his homosexuality, even to the extent, at the *Private Eye* lunches, of retailing strongly anti-homosexual gossip. As for the damaging anonymous letter to *Private Eye*, the only possible hint of homosexuality came with the sentence, 'Gone in his vintage Bentley . . . and his chauffeur, dear Jeffrey'; the rest was concerned with business affairs.

Yet by far the most curious aspect of Addey's blackmail story was its utter irrelevance to the main issue. Whatever Addey's motives in going to see Paisner — even supposing that Gillard was blackmailing him — it did not alter the main point of the story, namely Paisner's allegations of misconduct. The blackmail charge was quite gratuitous: its only possible use was to let Addey off whatever hook he was caught on, and to provide Goldsmith with another stick with which to beat *Private Eye*.

Why then did Addey make this statement, which was to prove so much more incriminating to him than anything that *Private Eye* could ever have published about him? His answer to me was probably in part true — i.e. that he had been pressured into it. But how? The threat he mentioned to me, of a Criminal Libel action against him by Goldsmith and Levine, was rather implausible, though it might have played a part in influencing him. Addey could indeed be said to have slandered Levine with his story of a bogus American client, but as the law stands there is no such thing as criminal slander, a fact that Addey, who read for the Bar, might be expected to know. In any case, on the basis of what Paisner had told him, Addey could easily have defended an action for slander.

But what of Paisner himself? His statement was, if anything, more mystifying still. Nothing was revealed in the affidavits about his behaviour between his interview with Goldsmith at Leadenhall Street on Thursday, 13 May, and the signing of the affidavit at his home four days later — except that, if Addey was to be believed, Paisner had spoken to him on Saturday and said his story was a 'pack of lies'. The strangest thing about it was its style, which smacked more of a confession in a Russian show trial than an affidavit from a senior solicitor — 'I am deeply ashamed of my own conduct. Only now do I fully understand . . . what harm and damage I have caused Eric Levine' etc.

It was perfectly possible, of course, that Paisner, knowing what he did about Levine, would indeed have resented the way in which the man had prospered. But the idea of Paisner being in the grip of a vindictive passion was completely at odds with the calm and collected figure that Marnham had spoken to. And, as with Addey, certain obvious discrepancies arose. Why, if Paisner's story was 'a pack of lies' did he, having spoken to Marnham, urge him to confirm as many details as he could from other sources, even going so far as to suggest names of people who might help? As soon as Marnham began to speak to these people he would surely have quickly found out that Paisner's story was quite untrue.

There were, too, some curious instances of wording in the affidavit. The expression 'pack of lies' was used three times. Paisner told Addey a 'pack of lies'; then Addey confessed to Paisner that his story of an American client was ' a pack of lies'. (This was, in fact, a direct quotation, as Addey, curiously, had used the identical expression in his letter to Paisner dictated in

65

Goldsmith's office.) Then Paisner reiterated that everything he had said to Addey and Marnham was 'a pack of lies'.

It was a strange expression for an elderly solicitor, accustomed all his life to pompous legal terminology, to use. Was there anything, we wondered, in the fact that it was also one of Goldsmith's own favourite expressions, employed to describe any statement with which he disagreed? (He was later to use it at Bow Street to describe the Elwes article.)

Again it was rather extraordinary that both Addey and Paisner, on quite separate occasions, admitted that they were 'deeply ashamed' of what they had done. 'I am deeply ashamed of my conduct', Addey had written in his letter to Paisner. 'I am deeply ashamed of my conduct', Paisner echoed in his affidavit, signed three days later.

These stylistic peculiarities, taken with the grovelling tone adopted by both men and the fact that Addey's letters were typed on Goldsmith's typewriter, and Paisner's on Levine's, suggested that their statements were to some extent dictated for them, either by Goldsmith, or Levine, or both.

Finally, as Gillard and I had to continue to remind ourselves, the most startling thing about these affidavits was the status of the two men who had signed them. Paisner and Addey were not frightened nobodies or novices. Both were tough, experienced and highly successful men. Paisner had acted for a number of tycoons like Sir Isaac Wolfson, and was therefore well accustomed to dealing with the rough-and-tumble of business life, whilst Addey, whose PR business was the largest in the country, had fought in the thick of many takeover battles. He had, for instance, advised Rupert Murdoch in his dramatic takeover bid for the *News of the World* which involved a long drawn-out struggle with the equally determined Robert Maxwell. Both these men, therefore, had experience of business life at its most ruthless.

So why had they signed such extraordinary statements? For the moment this, and many other questions, could not be answered. We could only surmise. But very soon, we thought, the truth would emerge, because when Goldsmith's application for an injunction was heard we could compel both men to come to court and be cross-examined. It was going to be an interesting case.

The Perils of Peerage

Whatever had happened to cause Addey's and Paisner's volte face, I had the strong feeling thereafter that Goldsmith, whose precise role in the Paisner/Addey affair was, and still is, unexplained, had now lost the whip hand. I was convinced from then on that somehow, whether in court or in print, the story would eventually rebound to his discredit, despite any temporary advantage he might gain over us.

Goldsmith, however, seemed to be of the opposite opinion. He spoke of having the 'trump card' and gave the impression of someone who could scarcely wait to get to court so that the facts could be revealed. From the beginning of the case he had had a bad press, and this had plainly surprised him, partly because he had, at the time, only the haziest ideas about Fleet Street and the sort of links *Private Eye* has with the rest of the press. Although newspaper proprietors and editors have strong reservations, to say the least, about the *Eye* — in our time we have been sued by the editors of almost every single national newspaper — the ordinary journalist tends to be a strong supporter. Partly this is because the magazine, from the start, has mocked the pretensions of Fleet Street itself. But the *Eye* has also acted as a reserve outlet for stories which, for a variety of reasons like fear of libel or the threat of withdrawal of advertising, has led to a close relationship between *Private Eye* and Fleet Street journalists. Some, like Nigel Dempster, are quite open about it; others have to be more secretive. Many contribute anonymously. Goldsmith seemed to have little understanding of these matters and, on finding himself under attack, assumed the existence of a sinister and powerful conspiracy arrayed against him, with tentacles stretching from our headquarters in Greek Street throughout all branches of the communications world.

The journalists involved had what he described, using his brother's ecological jargon, as a 'symbiotic relationship' with *Private Eye*. 'There are forty or fifty of them,' he told an American magazine, 'and you can find them through the media. They are extremists of left and right, and they have henchmen in Parliament, who are also of the extremist type. They are excellently co-ordinated. And they have used their columns to create an atmosphere around me.'

Now, however, without waiting to hear our side of the story, Goldsmith seemed to think he had acquired in Addey's affidavit a stick with which to beat *Private Eye* in the battle of public opinion. What could be better than to show that this magazine, apparently so highly thought of by so many unlikely people, went in for blackmail of the lowest sort in order to acquire its information? He could at last do something to influence those papers which had sided with the *Eye*.

There was, for instance, the *Spectator*, recently purchased by his friend, the young City millionaire, Henry Keswick, and now numbering one or two *Private Eye* writers like Auberon Waugh among its contributors. The *Spectator*, in its anonymous 'Notebook', had printed two or three fierce attacks on Goldsmith for suing *Private Eye*'s distributors. Goldsmith was soon on the phone to Keswick, warning him in excited tones to be more careful about his contributors. He told him the blackmail story in full.

And during the next few weeks Goldsmith lost no opportunity to spread the story around Fleet Street. He spoke to the editors of the *Times*, the *Daily Telegraph*, the *Sunday Express* and possibly others. His allies, like Harold Wilson and Lord Weidenfeld, seemed eager to pass the story on. In at least one instance, Goldsmith offered to show an editor the affidavits as proof of his charges.

This was another serious tactical mistake on Goldsmith's

part, for, whatever short-term gains might accrue, he was himself now running the risk of the very thing that Levine and Franklin had threatened Addey with, namely a slander action — in this case from Gillard, whom he was openly accusing of a criminal offence, blackmail.

An opportunity to do something about this came with the intervention in the story of the publisher Anthony Blond. Blond, a raffish and amusing figure who makes no secret of his homosexual connections, had been at Eton with Goldsmith and knew him and his family well; he was also, on the strength of his generous financial help in the lean years of *Private Eye* history, a director of the magazine. In fact, Blond had already given me some interesting information about his old school-friend. Goldsmith was, he said, a very superstitious man with a particular horror of rubber bands. Only recently he had been about to take off for Buenos Aires when he saw a rubber band lying on the floor of the aeroplane's first-class compartment. Goldsmith at once marched off the plane, closely followed by a group of Basque shepherds who, seeing that he was an important man, decided to follow his example.

Blond, like many others during the case, now took it upon himself to act as a mediator between his two warring friends. Would I object, he asked me, if he went to see Goldsmith? Not at all, I replied.

They met at Goldsmith's house in Tregunter Road on 24 May. Goldsmith, who always finds it difficult to remain still, paced up and down, jabbing a huge cigar to emphasise his points.

Private Eye, he said, were employing a journalist called Michael Gillard to dig up dirt on his lawyer, Eric Levine. He now had proof that Gillard had been blackmailing 'a professional man' — he did not name him.

Blond was naturally very upset to hear this and came round to the *Eye* the following day to suggest an immediate board meeting to discuss the Goldsmith case. I was not in the office that day but arranged for him to see Gillard and myself a few days later. We then explained the whole story to Blond and showed him the affidavits signed by Paisner and Addey. When he heard that the 'professional man' was John Addey, he roared with laughter. With his homosexual connections, Blond knew all about Addey — a sign that the latter's inclinations were fairly well known in such circles. No wonder that Goldsmith, guessing that Blond might not take an allegation from Addey so seriously, had talked solemnly and ambiguously about 'a professional man'.

Blond then agreed to make a statement himself, to be used in a possible slander action by Gillard. This cheered us up. To be in a position to counter-sue Goldsmith was an obvious step forward.

Meanwhile, Patrick Marnham and I had been trying to see if there was anything that could be discovered on the Lucan front. One difficulty was that it seemed as if the police themselves had been very wary in their approach to the Lucan set. Off the record, they complained to reporters about an 'Eton Mafia', but they had not taken the matter further. Goldsmith's name had cropped up very early in their investigations when they came across it in one of Lucan's bank accounts, which showed Goldsmith guaranteeing an overdraft of £5,000. They immediately rang his office with a request to see him, and though Goldsmith said in his affidavit that he 'readily and promptly complied', it had in fact been more than three weeks before the interview finally took place. The police, however, did not seem unduly resentful about this delay, and had apparently found Goldsmith very polite and charming when they spoke to him. 'It was almost as if he took over the interviewing', one of them was reported as saying. Both men, Detective Chief Superintendent Roy Ranson and Detective Inspector David Gerring, were well aware of Goldsmith's links with Harold Wilson.

We made other enquiries. An interview with Lady Lucan proved fascinating, if not exactly helpful. Marnham and I called on her at Lower Belgrave Street on 21 May. We went up to the sitting room on the first floor. The room was cold and rather

71

shabby, the once grand furniture bursting at the seams. The most striking thing in the room was a large oil painting of her husband by Dominic Elwes, which stood in front of the fire place. The portrait, in an ornate gilded frame with 'The Earl of Lucan by Dominic Elwes' pinned below on a little plaque, showed Lucan in peer's robes, standing in the same sort of pose in which the Queen was painted by Annigoni. But Lucan's face, in this grand setting, looked utterly incongruous. It was pallid and sickly, as though he was suffering from an awful hangover. The painting illustrated graphically the two sides of Elwes's personality — the rampant snobbery and the acute observation of reality.

Set up in pride of place, the painting seemed like a symbol of Lady Lucan's ambivalent attitude towards her murderer husband. Why should she continue to display his portrait if she did not to some extent still idolise him, in spite of all that had occurred? Like Elwes, she was the victim of destructive snobbery, but, like Elwes, she was absolutely truthful. A small, rather pretty figure, she sat on a settee — she had obviously made a great effort to look smart for the occasion — speaking quite lucidly about her experiences. Her attitude towards her persecutors was one of defiance, and in spite of all our differences she obviously felt some sympathy for *Private Eye*, as both of us had been subjected to a course of hounding, though by different people. Her solicitor sat with her throughout. She described Elwes's visit to her in hospital; how he had been 'boringly insistent' on seeing her although she was sedated at the time, and how he had burst into tears when she told him not only that Lucan had done the murder, but that she had told the police as much.

However, Veronica Lucan could tell us little about Goldsmith. She and her husband had been to stay with him several times at his house on the Riviera, but apart from that she had only seen him at the Clermont Club.

All this time we had been expecting the Levine injunction hearing to come to court. But a series of legal delays, of the type which the layman finds it impossible to understand, held up the hearing. The original *ex parte* application had been on 18 May, on which occasion I had been told that the case would come up in a few days. In fact it was not until the beginning of July that we finally went to court. Meanwhile, we were bound by our undertaking not to mention Goldsmith or Levine in *Private Eye*.

One irritating consequence of this, which Goldsmith may or may not have foreseen, was that *Private Eye* was unable to comment on his inclusion in Harold Wilson's Honours List when it was finally published. In view, however, of the storm that erupted from every other quarter, our silence on this occasion could have been of little comfort to him.

Since the *Daily Express*'s 'It's LORD GOLDSMITH!' story of 19 May, there had been several developments. On 23 May, the *Sunday Times*, emboldened, now produced a much more informative article. The honours that had been queried by the Scrutiny Committee were:

> James Goldsmith (peerage);
> Sir Jospeh Kagan (peerage);
> Jarvis Astaire (knighthood).

This latest leak, the most authoritative to date, led not only to a government enquiry being set up into how the names got out, but also to a widespread demand in Parliament and the press that there should be no further delay in the official publication of the full list. It was finally published a few days later, on 27 May. It included peerages for Lew Grade, Bernard Delfont, and George Weidenfeld, and a knighthood for Eric Miller. Of the three that had been queried, Kagan got by with his peerage, Astaire got nothing at all, and Goldsmith was demoted to a knight. His citation stated: 'For services to exports and ecology'. This wording in itself was peculiar, for exports formed in fact only a tiny percentage (0.4%) of the Cavenham output, whilst it was his brother Teddy who had performed services to ecology.

73

The uproar that followed the publication of the list outdid any other in Wilson's career, so much so that he never really recovered from it. Many commentators fell back on excretory metaphors. 'It stinks like a sewer lorry', John Junor, the editor of the *Sunday Express*, said on the radio programme *Any Questions?*, while one cabinet minister summed up the view of a lot of Labour Party members when he said: 'Such a graceful exit. And then he had to go and do this on the doorstep.'

Despite her shrill denials, there could be little doubt that Marcia Williams was responsible for the more controversial names — a fact that was later confirmed by Wilson's press secretary, Joe Haines, in his book *The Politics of Power*. George Weidenfeld was her publisher and regular escort; John Vaizey, another peer, was her admirer and had apparently helped to get her two sons entered for a public school. Goldsmith and Miller had both on separate occasions been spotted dancing with her at Annabel's; and however much she protested in a long and incoherent letter to *The Times* about anti-Semitism, part of her had obviously foreseen and was enjoying the furore. It was indeed a repetition of her own elevation to the peerage two years before. There had been an outcry on that occasion, too, but she had plainly relished being able to cock a snook at her enemy the press, including *Private Eye*, the magazine that had first revealed the existence of her two illegitimate children. We could all sneer and jibe as much as we liked, but she was still Lady Falkender; and now, likewise, her friends were *Lord* Weidenfeld and *Sir* James Goldsmith. It was, too, a way of asserting her power over the Queen, who had been forced in the end to give her assent to the list with only minimal changes. The pleasure that Lady Falkender derived from all this was no doubt the more welcome since it helped to compensate for the knowledge that she herself, once Wilson had resigned, was now virtually powerless — which was why she had moved heaven and earth to stop him going.

Goldsmith, however, like Wilson, enjoyed it less. Although he had assured his friend Sam White that a knighthood was actually more use to him than a peerage in his forthcoming political career, the opposite was in fact the case. A peerage was a short cut to Parliament, to Westminster, where he had been hoping to 'participate' in some vague and undefined way. With the help of a peerage he could even have become a minister, like for example Lord Brayley, an obscure businessman friend of Wilson's who had risen to become Minister for the Army before his hurriedly enforced resignation in 1974.

In addition to the humiliating demotion from his original peerage, Goldsmith was now subjected to a storm of abuse and ridicule, especially from Labour MPs, a hundred of whom signed a motion condemning the list. All the critics seemed to focus especially on him. 'The name that was causing most astonishment and anger', the *Daily Telegraph* lobby correspondent reported on the day of the list's publication, 'was that of Sir James Goldsmith.'

Why was this so? The list, after all, contained many equally incongruous names. There was James Hanson, for example, another financier, and, like Goldsmith, a Tory benefactor. But his honour slipped by almost unnoticed. More remarkable, in retrospect, was the lack of attention given at the time to the Chairman of the Peachey Property Corporation, Eric Miller, who had been made a knight. (Miller was to shoot himself sixteen months later, his career in ruins, and the prospect of imprisonment ahead of him.)

It was said that the anti-Goldsmith resentment sprang from the fact that he was known as a Tory supporter. But although it was Labour MPs who protested, it was the Tory papers like the *Sunday Express* and the *Daily Telegraph* who attacked him most fiercely. The *Daily Mail* described him as 'Lord Lucan's gambling crony', and several leader writers echoed Lord Crathorne of the Scrutiny Committee, who had said: 'We couldn't see what the fellers had done for Britain. We didn't like the cut of their jib.'

In fact, however, Goldsmith had done no more and no less for Britain than most of the nonentities who get honoured by political parties. There can be no doubt that a major cause of this upsurge of feeling against him was his campaign against *Private Eye*. It was mainly for this that he was well known. Until he sued *Private Eye*, Goldsmith was a relatively obscure figure. Gossip column readers remembered him vaguely in connection with the Patino and Lucan affairs; stockbrokers and investors had followed the ups and downs, not to mention the sidesteps, of Cavenham; but to the general public, even the press, he was virtually unknown. It was by suing *Private Eye* for Criminal Libel that he had made the fatal mistake of becoming conspicuous. He had attracted the hostility of the press by seemingly using his great power and wealth to crush a small magazine; he had also, in the curious way that things happen in this country that he wished to sort out but so little understood, offended many members of the old guard by trying to do away with the court jester. The result was that when the Honours List was published it was his name that was seized on as a symbol of all that was rotten about it, while Eric Miller, who kept his head down but was much more deserving of brickbats than Goldsmith, got through without a murmur.

In any case, whoever took the fatal step and demoted Goldsmith from peer to knight — whether it was James Callaghan or even the Queen herself — had dealt a final blow to his political ambitions. With no peerage, and Wilson gone, and with Honours List mud all over his face, Sir James Goldsmith had no hope, in the immediate future at least, of 'participating' at Westminster.

It was nice to think that *Private Eye* had played an important part in this reversal. And yet the mystery remained. Why had Goldsmith been singled out for an honour? Most of the other names on the list were those of old friends and cronies. But Goldsmith had known Wilson and Falkender for only a few months and it was impossible to point to any services rendered by him apart, apparently, from some words of advice about the French economy.

Somewhere there had to be an explanation.

76

The Injunction Hearing

From the *Eye*'s point of view, this incident of the Honours List was an enormous boost, because it linked Goldsmith in the public mind with Harold Wilson. Up till then he had been the lone financier fighting, for motives that were unclear, his own private war. But now many people who had not followed the story very closely rallied to *Private Eye*'s side solely because the man we were up against was revealed to be a friend and ally of Harold Wilson and Lady Falkender.

From that point on the campaign became a bit of a crusade against whatever it was that the Honours List stood for. Students launched their own appeals, MPs and branches of the National Union of Students passed the hat round. Sir Max Aitken's daughter, Kirsty, organised with her friend, Caroline Cowan, a discotheque at the Chelsea Football Club which raised £1,500. A further contribution came from a 'Golden Ball' given at her house in Chiswick by Philippa Allen, wife of an ex-Wilson aide, John Schofield Allen.

In response to our own appeal for funds to fight the case, hundreds of letters and cheques poured into Greek Street from all sorts of people. A list of names selected at random gives some idea of those who contributed:

'Tiny' Rowland; Anthony Sampson; Deptford Labour Party; the Earl of Lichfield; *Northern Echo* subs; Prof H.R. Trevor-Roper; Johnny Morris; Baroness Wooton of Abinger; Simon Dee; Dept. of Chemical Pathology, St Bart's Hospital; 'All the staff at WH Smith, Kingsway (except the manager)'; Sir Alec Guinness; 'Five King's Lynn solicitors'; Ampleforth College; Shields and District NUJ.

An anonymous note on House of Lords writing paper read: '£20 for Goldenballs Fund. From a supposedly wealthy but in fact very impoverished peer. You can record it as from a member of HM Privy Council who prefers open justice to money!'

A London taxi-driver wrote:

'I am a London tax-driver. I have never in my twenty-eight years on this earth found any reason to donate anything other than scepticism to any so-called cause or appeal, excluding certain charities. I often read *Private Eye* and sometimes I am amused, amazed at your revelations, shocked at your lack of concern at some of the undoubtable inexactitudes and disgusted by your sometimes obscene phraseology. However I will be damned if I will allow any one man to stifle one of the very few politically or economically uncontrolled magazines left in this country.'

Such letters were very heartening, even if I sometimes felt tempted to take the advice of a 'Doctor in Leeds' who wrote to me:

'I feel that the time has come that this country no longer deserves people like yourself, who are prepared to stick their necks out against the general rot that goes on day by day. What you are doing is appreciated by only a tiny majority of people, even among the readership of *Private Eye*. *Private Eye* has brought me an immense amount of pleasure but in spite of this I would say now that the best thing you could do, for yourself and your family, would be to throw in the towel and go out and buy a farm somewhere or something like that. Let the bloody bankers and lawyers and everyone else see how they get on without you tipping them off all the time.'

Meanwhile we had still not been given a date for the injunction hearing, and as the weeks went by, to Gillard and myself it looked more and more as if Eric Levine was deliberately dragging his feet in order to continue to take advantage of our undertaking not to mention him. Not only had we been prevented from writing about Goldsmith's knighthood, there were now further developments at Slater Walker which Gillard was keen to comment on. Yet we were debarred from doing so. To protests from Geoffrey Bindman, Levine replied that he was still waiting for an affidavit from Gillard, giving his version of the Addey story; yet it was our view that submission of an affidavit would lead to further delay while they sought even more 'information' from Addey. Impatience in the end got the better of us, and we printed a piece on Slater Walker and Goldsmith's settlement of the Haw Par affair, though we did not mention him by name. This turned out to be a costly mistake.

At long last the case was set down to be heard on Monday, 5 July, and we began to make final preparations. Affidavits had been obtained from most of the people at the *Private Eye* lunch who had listened to Addey talking merrily away about Goldsmith and Levine. Normally I dread the approach of a court case and my heart sinks when I enter the mock-Gothic cathedral of the Law Courts, walking down the long echoing passages past the little knots of lawyers clustered with their clients waiting for their cases to begin, but for once I found myself looking forward to the hearing with something approaching excitement. We had a strong hand. And it would be fascinating to see how Paisner and Addey explained themselves. It was therefore in a spirit of eager anticipation that we assembled outside the court. Our QC, James Comyn, bewigged, gowned and puffing at his Sweet Afton, seemed pretty confident.

The atmosphere of this occasion was further enlivened by Goldsmith's presence in court. He sat on the front bench beside Eric Levine, and in the lunch-break the two of them could be seen pacing the corridor, Goldsmith towering over the diminutive lawyer — the two of them looking, as Gillard said, like Mutt and Jeff. It was the first opportunity we had to observe Goldsmith at close quarters. A tall, restless, nail-biting man, expensively dressed, he looked at least ten years older than forty-three. His face was tanned, his eyes a steely blue. In repose, his expression was peculiarly dead. But his face would frequently crinkle into a smile and — which was disconcerting — from time to time he looked across at me, nodding and grinning, as if trying to convey a message of some kind.

The judge, Mr Justice Donaldson, had gained some notoriety a year or two previously when he rashly agreed to preside over the Tory government's disastrous Industrial Relations Court, the aim of which had been to make the unions conform to the rule of law, but which ended with him being forced to send the leaders of the dockers' union to prison. One could see at once why the Tories had selected him, for he was a quiet and reasonable man without any pomposity, the last person trade union leaders could dismiss as a traditional old die-hard judge or establishment stooge.

After a cursory look through the papers, Donaldson began, as apparently he often did, by asking if there was not some way in which the case could be settled out of court without a costly hearing. We then all went into a huddle. But it emerged that the Goldsmith terms had not been modified. He was still insisting on the undertaking not to mention Levine and the forty-eight hour vetting procedure. The case would have to go ahead.

The next day it was revealed that John Addey, who had been informed the previous Friday that his presence would be required in court, had gone to Italy, leaving no forwarding address. As he had not been served with a subpoena compelling his attendance, he was apparently within his rights. All that Donaldson would say about this vanishing act was that it was 'unfortunate'. For obvious reasons, I found this description of Addey's behaviour inadequate.

On the evening of that same Tuesday, the second day of the hearing, a subpoena was served on Paisner to attend the following day. But on Wednesday morning we were surprised to find a QC called John Wilmers, another heavyweight like Hawser, who announced to the judge that he was representing Paisner and would like to call the latter's doctor, Nigel Southward, to give evidence.

In the witness box the doctor said that his fellow practitioner, Dr Sturridge, had been called to see Paisner at nine o'clock the previous evening (i.e. following the delivery of the subpoena) and had found his patient 'extremely confused and disorientated . . . . He looked ill and exhausted and kept repeating that he just wanted to sleep'. Southward had himself attended Paisner that morning. He was lying motionless in bed. 'He kept saying he wanted to end it all.'

I looked at Levine. He was smiling. I couldn't help remembering Dominic Elwes.

Dr Southward added that Paisner had been suffering from acute depression at the end of May, about two weeks, that is, before he made his 'confession' on 16 May.

So that was it. Our two witnesses had failed to materialise and the case would continue without them. That afternoon I found myself in the witness box, facing a barrage of questions from Lewis Hawser.

Throughout this case Hawser knew that he was on weak legal ground. He therefore used the occasion partly to fish up as much information as he could, for use in future cases. He had already announced that Goldsmith was going to bring Contempt of Court proceedings against Gillard and myself for breaking our undertaking, and he was thinking ahead to this. He asked to cross-examine all the defendants — myself, Gillard, Marnham, Dempster, Waugh and West.

Hawser's main line was that *Private Eye* — 'a magazine quite reckless in its attacks, my Lord' — had been about to publish the details of Levine's misdemeanours at Paisner's and that we had only been restrained from doing so by their application for an injunction, which must now be granted at all costs. This, of course, was not true. In line with Paisner's own advice, and knowing the obvious perils of printing the story, we were engaged in the process of trying to check the details wherever possible from other sources. In any case, our main interest in the Paisner story was as ammunition in the Levine libel action.

Now, however, from a purely journalistic point of view, the position had altered. The story of Paisner and Addey, culminating in their failure to turn up in court that morning, was obviously a much better 'story' than anything about what Levine had or had not been doing during his time at Paisner's. Lawyers, however, do not look at things in terms of 'stories', and I don't think this point had occurred to Hawser. All of them seemed to think, or at least hope, that the proceedings being *in camera*, there was no reason why anything should ever get out about what had happened.

Hawser wisely steered clear of the Paisner side of the story and concentrated on Addey. Goldsmith had plainly persuaded himself that the blackmail story was true, and though Hawser may have had his doubts on this score, he seemed to be under instructions to pursue an aggressive line on the subject.

During my own cross-examination we gained one interesting insight into Addey's behaviour. Out of the blue, Hawser asked me if I had had a meeting with him on 19 May. After a few moments' puzzlement, I realised that this must be a reference to our final encounter at the Albany, the one we both agreed 'had not taken place'. I said that I had indeed met him. If Hawser knew about it, there seemed no point in denying it further.

Hawser then asked me: 'Did you say that if Addey did not recant, Gillard would destroy him?' I had said no such thing, of course, but the question suggested that Addey had been in touch with Levine after he had signed his affidavit and given him a fictitious account of our conversation. Levine would then have asked him to put it in writing for them. Addey must have refused. At which point Levine presumably decided that Addey was of no more use to them, and was probably quite relieved when he did his disappearing act.

Still, Hawser was unwilling to let the Addey blackmail story go. One fact that he and Goldsmith found difficult to accept was that we had all been ignorant of Addey's homosexuality. Hawser was even prepared to accuse me of lying about this. It was Gillard who later pointed out to him that it was perfectly possible to know someone very well and at the same time not to know some quite important fact about him, should he choose to conceal it. Donaldson himself intervened to say that the spy Vassall had been the classic case of a man who was well known as a homosexual in homosexual circles and had managed to keep it from others. But still Hawser persisted with this line, putting it to Auberon Waugh:

> Q. I suggest that it was really a very remarkable situation in that it was quite well known in certain circles that Addey is a homosexual but none of the *Private Eye* people who swore affidavits in this case say that it ever crossed their minds.
>
> A. Well, I don't find it as odd as you do in my own case because I don't move in homosexual circles, and he had none of the usual characteristics of a homosexualist — he didn't wiggle his bottom, he didn't talk with a lisp, he didn't wear scent, and I had no reason to suppose that he was anything but perfectly normal.

Waugh's appearance in the box, which, unlike me, he thoroughly enjoyed, brought home what a great mistake Goldsmith made by roping him into the affair. He had done so partly because of the notion of a *Private Eye* conspiracy, a notion that gained ground in his mind and made him talk later about a closely-knit group of extremists, led by me, 'excellently co-ordinated', using their columns to 'create an atmosphere . . . .

like a drip feeding pus into the system'. Goldsmith was convinced that Waugh must have had a hand in the anonymous pro-*Eye* pieces that had appeared in the *Spectator*. (In fact, they were written by an ex-barrister, Simon Courtauld, who at the time I had not even met.) Once served with a writ, Waugh, who had until then been remarkably restrained on the subject of Goldsmith, penned a piece of ferocious abuse which I think was probably the only article in the course of the whole affair which caused Goldsmith real distress. It appeared in the *Spectator* on 5 June under the title 'Trying to be Fair', and read in part as follows:

> 'My reflections on the most suitable Englishman to lead the country out of its present decline were interrupted by a telephone call from a firm of solicitors: someone called Mr James Goldsmith (as he then was) proposed to seek a High Court injunction restraining me from any adverse comment about himself, or his solicitor and friend, a gentleman called Mr Eric Levine, while they proceeded with a writ for Criminal Libel against *Private Eye*.
>
> For some time I puzzled over why I should be singled out from the whole field of British journalists as the one most likely to inspire prejudice against Goldsmith and Levine. There are already perfectly adequate laws against such behaviour, and the laws of libel are more than adequate to deal with any defamatory falsehoods I might have in mind. I am not, and never have been, an employee of *Private Eye* — it is just one of five newspapers and magazines to which I contribute regular signed articles, and it provides much less than a fifth of my earned income from writing. I do not think I have ever met Goldsmith or written about him, and I am reasonably certain that I have never met or written about Levine. Neither suggests that I have ever libelled him.
>
> Yet now I must hire lawyers and sit down to compose

an affidavit, or possibly drag myself to London from West Somerset, losing two days' work in the process, to explain why I should be allowed to pass adverse comment on these two people if I choose. It is one of the scandals of our society that only the very rich or the penniless can afford to go to the law, unless they are prepared to stake their fortune on what may prove no better chance than the toss of a coin . . .

There is a strong temptation not to defend the case at all and let the little fellow have his injunction if that is what he wants. After all, I have spent the last fifteen years as a journalist without once feeling the urge to make adverse comments on Mr Goldsmith or his fat friend, and it should not be too difficult to restrain myself for a little longer. But in the few weeks remaining before the plea for an injunction is heard, I find a strange fretfulness come over me. Hold a cat by the tail, and however happy it may have been standing on the spot before, it will be prepared to pull its tail out by the roots in its anxiety to go somewhere else immediately. Obviously, I must use these weeks of freedom to pass as many adverse comments as I can think of, so long as they are: (1) not libellous, and (2) unlikely to influence a jury. It is not easy, because I have never met the fellow, as I say, and know practically nothing about him. But I have seen his photograph in the newspapers, and the first thing that needs to be said is that he has a disgustingly ugly face.

Looking at that dreadful face, I can't imagine, personally, what a nice, well-brought-up English girl like Annabel Birley sees there, but it is one of the tragedies of my life that the nicest, cleverest and most attractive women see qualities in other men which I can't see at all. You can't judge a girl by the men she chooses. Perhaps these men are exceptionally good in bed — not a quality to endear them to their own sex, whether it derives from greater agility, staying power, passion, tenderness, or simply the possession of a larger organ.

There are those who say that size doesn't count, and in any case I am not sure it would be proper to speculate on the size of Mr Goldsmith's organ at the present time. Under normal circumstances, it would be safe to assume that he has one, and even (on the principle that a cat may look at a king) to speculate about its size, but as soon as a man starts issuing writs for libel he immediately assumes many of the properties of an angel; his body is no longer a weak, farting, nose-picking thing we all recognise as a human body, but emerges in its glorified and resurrected state without spot or blemish.

Such speculations might even be held likely to influence a jury in criminal proceedings (the women jurors taking one point of view, perhaps, the men another) and that is something which I understandably wish to avoid at all costs. So perhaps I had better confine my adverse comment to the proposition that Sir James Goldsmith has a repulsively ugly face. So, it happens, does Mr Eric Levine, but these are only expressions of a personal opinion which a jury will be able to judge for themselves, if they think it relevant . . .'

Goldsmith seemed to enjoy the cross-examination of Waugh and the rest of us. Neglecting his business for a whole week, he sat through every minute of the hearing, apparently enthralled, as though it were a piece of theatre he had mounted for his own entertainment. I remember that while giving evidence, with Goldsmith sitting on the front bench below grinning in that disconcerting way of his, I had the strong feeling that he was slightly intrigued by all of us and was in a way envious of my own position — that he would have liked, in other words, to be editor of *Private Eye*.

The appearance of Gillard, however, in the witness box, was a more serious affair. Gillard obviously had a very thorough knowledge of Goldsmith's business activities. He had also by now mustered enough evidence to sue Addey and Goldsmith for slander. It proved rather difficult, however, to find a firm of solicitors willing to take on the case. Three firms, including his own solicitors, turned it down before the left-wing lawyer, Ben Birnberg, agreed to handle it. Now we had the satisfaction of seeing this firm's emissary deliver a letter to Goldsmith informing him of the writ during the hearing. He opened it, gave a rather mirthless smile and passed it over to Levine. The writ was reported in the *Richmond Herald* under the pleasing headline, 'Local Man Sues Millionaire'.

And now, with Gillard in the witness box, there occurred another odd twist to the hearing, which derived from a visit which Anthony Blond had made to *Private Eye* some days before.

Blond had asked if he could take away copies of the Paisner and Addey affidavits to show to his lawyer. The only ones to hand were those on which Gillard had scrawled a number of notes. This didn't seem to matter, and we made copies of them. Then Blond, when he wrote out his statement for our use in the slander action, had asked his lawyer to send a copy of it to Goldsmith. But for some reason the copies of Paisner's and Addey's affidavits which we had provided to Blond were also sent and in this way papers covered with Gillard's annotations, which by now after several copyings were almost illegible, had come into the hands of Goldsmith and Levine.

Inexplicably, the other side seemed to regard this as a great stroke of luck. Apparently convinced that the notes contained incriminating material, Hawser made Gillard decipher word for word what he had written. In fact, Gillard, with his habitual thoroughness, had just jotted down, in his own shorthand form, every little error and inconsistency contained in Addey's affidavit. The result was that, in spite of Addey's absence, we were given an excellent opportunity to show how riddled with holes his story was.

When Dick West's turn came to give evidence, Hawser was once more made to look ridiculous. He had already put it to me very definitely that I had commissioned what he called 'a total exposure' of Eric Levine from Dick West, and we were wondering how he had got this idea so firmly in his head. It eventually emerged that his source was an unnamed person who claimed to have overheard Dick talking to some journalists in El Vino's one day early in May. (Dick had, in fact, offered the *Spectator* a piece on the property deals of Levine and T. Dan Smith in Northampton. But it contained no new information and was rejected.)

In spite of these setbacks, Hawser succeeded in making a very powerful closing speech, once again piling point on point, and building a convincing picture of the poor litigant, Goldsmith, seeking his redress before the courts and being simultaneously harried by a pack of malicious journalists seeking to pressure him into premature surrender. Had we not already shown by our breach of the undertaking that we were utterly reckless and uncontrollable? Only an injunction would stop further outrages. Paisner and Addey were quite forgotten as he pounded on with his talk of 'opprobrious attacks' and 'vilification', and at the end of it our junior, Desmond Browne, was pessimistic about our chance of winning.

It fell to Desmond on this occasion to make the closing speech for our side, in the unavoidable absence of James Comyn. His main argument was that, no matter how many writs Goldsmith had issued, no matter how many attacks there had been on him in *Private Eye*, we could not be compelled by law to shut up about him, let alone Levine, who had not even threatened to sue. Goldsmith's view seemed to be that, once a libel writ, or in his case about a hundred libel writs, had been issued, the matter became *sub judice* until the case was heard; in other words, until the Criminal Libel case had been resolved, and the civil cases decided, a process which could take as long as two years, *Private Eye* was in Contempt of Court if we continued to write about him. But this was not the law, which was firmly opposed to the principle of the so-called gagging writ. The matter had been clearly stated by Lord Justice Salmon in *Thomson v Times Newspapers* (1969), in one of those clear and sensible judgements which occasionally pierce through legal waffle in law reports:

'It is a widely held fallacy [Salmon had said] that the issue of a writ automatically stifles further comment. There is no authority that I know of to support the view that further comment would amount to a contempt of court. Once a newspaper has justified, and there is some *prima facie* support for the justification, the Plaintiff cannot obtain an interlocutory injunction to restrain the Defendant from repeating the matters complained of. In these circumstances, it is obviously wrong to suppose they would be committing a contempt of court by doing so. It seems to me equally obvious that no newspaper that repeats the same sort of criticism is committing a contempt of court. They may be publishing libel, and if they do so, and they have no defence to it, they will have to pay whatever may be the appropriate damages. But the writ does not, in my view, preclude the publication of further criticism; it merely puts the person who makes the further criticism at risk of being sued for libel; and he takes the same risk whether or not there has been any previous publication. I appreciate that very often newspapers are chary about repeating criticism when a writ for libel has been issued because they feel they are running some risk of being proceeded against for contempt. Without expressing my final view, because the point is not before this court for decision, I think that in this they are mistaken. No doubt the law relating to contempt could and should be clarified in this respect.'

Of course in our own case we had not repeated or even threatened to repeat the libel, i.e. the Lucan allegation or the so-called 'intriguing link' with T. Dan Smith. What Goldsmith thought we were going to do was publish Paisner's story, though he had no way of proving it.

Donaldson gave his judgement on 16 July. He began, like almost every judge in the affair, by proclaiming his unshaken belief in the freedom of the press. But though the abstract concept of press freedom appeals to judges, when they see something like *Private Eye* that embodies the idea in practice, they do not like it. From time to time Donaldson, in his courteous way, had indicated that he thought *Private Eye* went too far. I don't think he particularly enjoyed Waugh's *Spectator* piece and he obviously failed to take a shine to Nigel Dempster.

At the same time, he had plainly grasped the significance of the Paisner/Addey incident. He had said himself, of the Paisner affidavit: 'I have to say that when I first read it my reaction was, Is the man mad? Or has someone twisted his arm?' Obviously Donaldson thought that the affair should not be allowed to rest where it did; on the other hand, as it seemed to me, he did not particularly want me to carry out my plan, as hinted, of writing the whole thing up in *Private Eye*. But the fact that the judgement was in public, and could be quoted by the newspapers, gave him the opportunity to let the story out. He therefore prefaced his judgement with a long and detailed account of what had happened.

Going on to legal argument, Donaldson showed himself to be a sensible rather than a clever judge — that is, he came to the right decision by rather convoluted reasoning. He seemed to accept Salmon on the gagging writ, and went on to point out that it was difficult for the courts to prohibit the publication of something unless they knew in advance what it was. In the absence of any specific text, apart from Dick West's unpublished *Spectator* article, what Goldsmith was applying for was a general injunction to stop us committing Contempt of Court. But this was absurd, because we were bound in any case not to commit Contempt of Court and would do so at our peril. He therefore dismissed the application, while concluding with a few words of warning addressed to me and amounting to 'Watch your step'.

Goldsmith, who was ordered to pay the costs of the seven-day hearing, was not in court to hear the judgement. But as reporters filed out, they were handed a press-release saying he would appeal against Donaldson's judgement; that he was issuing yet another writ in respect of *Private Eye*'s article about Haw Par; that he would be suing Gillard and myself for breaking our undertaking; and that he would defend Gillard's slander action, doing everything in his power to see that it came to court quickly.

Asked to comment by an *Evening Standard* reporter, I said I thought Goldsmith had gone 'right over the top'.

A Matter of Contempt

There were times during that wonderful summer of 1976, the year which was so hot and dry that the government appointed a Minister of Drought, when we seemed to be in court almost every week.

To begin with, on 29 July, there were committal proceedings for Criminal Libel at Bow Magistrates Court. From a legal point of view, it was a formality; there was no hope of the Chief Magistrate overruling the earlier verdict that this was a criminal case. The occasion was treated more as a social one. The tiny courtroom was crammed with reporters. Goldsmith surprised the press by appearing for the first time in public with Lady Annabel Birley on his arm, thus sparking off rumours that they were about to get married, and Aspinall also turned up to lend moral support.

This was the only time during the affair that Goldsmith gave evidence in person. It was very diverting. James Comyn, asking questions in his soft Irish voice, managed to provoke him almost to a frenzy. As he paced up and down the narrow witness box, like one of Aspinall's tigers, his voice rose to a high pitch and he spat out his words with contempt. The idea of a Lucan circle was ' a total nonsense and fabrication'. What did he think of the Elwes part of the story, which he hadn't sued over? 'I regard it as typical of the filth of this magazine.'

'Isn't your aim to smash *Private Eye*?' Comyn asked quietly.

'No,' Goldsmith snarled, leaning across and jabbing his finger at me, 'I only want them to be more TRUTHFUL!'

'Do you mind behaving a little less theatrically, Sir James?' the magistrate, Mr Kenneth Barraclough, asked.

Afterwards, Annabel Birley could be heard congratulating him. 'You were F.E. Smith reincarnated', she said, and Aspinall added loyally: 'I think we got them with both barrels.'

Two weeks later I was in court again, charged with Gillard of Contempt of Court. There was no doubt that, owing to my failure to appreciate the wide terms and legal force of the temporary undertaking not to mention Levine or Goldsmith, we had breached it on four occasions, although three of these involved trivial references. The fourth breach was Gillard's article on the Haw Par settlement. But in the light of Judge Donaldson's verdict, rejecting Goldsmith's injunction, our own QC, James Comyn, regarded the offence as 'a very technical contempt', and advised us to acknowledge our guilt and apologise to the court in advance. We did so, and in the event were fined £250 apiece.

Before this contempt case came on, I had been passed a message via Nigel Dempster from a source of his at Eric Levine's office. The message was, roughly: 'Tell Ingrams to watch out. He will soon realise that we've got a spy in his camp.' The meaning of this became clear when we received Goldsmith's document for the case a few days later. They included photostats of three of Gillard's 'Slicker' manuscripts, which Levine now produced to prove that he had written items on Goldsmith, including the Haw Par piece. These papers could only have come from *Private Eye*.

The spy propaganda certainly had its effect, and I realised then that there is nothing more demoralising than the thought that someone whose loyalty you take completely for granted might be a traitor. You look with new eyes on people who have been working for you for years, and begin to harbour suspicions about them. Others, who have grudges against their colleagues, foster the rumour.

After thinking it over, however, I was convinced that the spy story could not be true. The Gillard manuscripts spanned a period of about eight months. If someone at *Private Eye* had been passing him material for that long, Goldsmith would have been extremely well-informed about us. But from Hawser's performance in the Donaldson case — the man in El Vino's etc. — it was obvious that Goldsmith's knowledge of our affairs was very primitive. It followed that the papers must have been stolen, either from inside the building or from the dustbins outside. If from the inside, it would have involved at least three separate break-ins, which seemed unlikely. The most plausible explanation was the dustbin one.

In court, this led to further sparring with Hawser. Desmond Browne asked to cross-examine Goldsmith to find out how he had acquired the articles. But Goldsmith, it was revealed, had now gone on holiday to Corsica. After prevaricating for some time, Hawser then admitted that 'a highly reputable firm of private investigators' had been employed to take papers from the dustbin. This would amount to theft, Desmond Browne said. No. Hawser replied, they had taken the papers out of the dustbin, made photocopies and then put them back. There was great amusement at this, and Desmond Browne said it would have saved a lot of time if Hawser had 'come clean' about the matter earlier. Hawser, by now furious, insisted on Desmond apologising for this dreadful slur on his character.

The use of private detectives was not new as far as Goldsmith was concerned. He had employed them in 1971 to try to sabotage Richard Milner's attack on him in the *Sunday Times*. Early in 1976, he had also offered their assistance to Harold Wilson to 'de-bug' his house at Great Missenden. (Wilson was at the time worried about a series of break-ins and the theft of papers.)

It occurred to me that if they could 'de-bug', these snoopers of Goldsmith's could 'bug' as well. But there was never any sign that they had done so. All they appeared to have done was to remove the *Private Eye* waste paper over a period of several months. But without the help of an interpreter, the material was of little use. Levine had told one journalist who phoned to make an enquiry: 'We have definite proof that you are the *Private Eye* informer.' But when Goldsmith, in an angry but unpublished letter to *The Times*, named another journalist as one of our 'paid informants', he got the wrong man and received a libel writ.

The dustbin affair made me take more seriously something I heard at the time — that Harold Wilson, lunching with a newspaper editor shortly after his resignation, had offered to supply him with a list of *Private Eye* informers. Horrified at what names might be revealed, the editor had refused the offer.

At a later stage I was to think of this story again. But meanwhile, as the sun shone and the grass turned brown, our legal battle with Goldsmith continued.

And now the nature of the battle had changed. For once the committal proceedings were over, the Criminal Libel case, which lawyers did not expect to come up for almost a year, was forgotten. Lucan, Elwes and Slater Walker were put to one side. As far as I was concerned, the issue now was whether *Private Eye* would or would not be 'gagged' in the interim.

The courts had refused to grant Goldsmith an injunction, and our undertaking had automatically lapsed once Donaldson gave his judgement; there was therefore no legal bar to prevent us writing about Goldsmith or Levine. On the other hand, Donaldson had warned me of the perils, unspecified, incurred when a paper showed an 'obsessional interest in a single matter of alleged public concern', and my lawyers advised strongly that it would be prudent for *Private Eye* to lay off Goldsmith for an indefinite period.

That was all very well. But meanwhile the Paisner/Addey story was left in the air. If Donaldson had hoped that the press would follow it up, he was disappointed. This was not surprising. The reporting of legal cases is in any event a very haphazard affair. More often than not the papers rely on a single agency man, which explains why they usually use identical wording in their reports. If his attention wanders, important points can go completely unreported. In the Donaldson case, after a long hearing in private, journalists were let in only for the judgement. Listening to the complicated story for the first time, they could hardly be expected to grasp its significance.

The next day only *The Times* gave the Paisner/Addey affair any coverage. The other papers seemed to think that Donaldson's warning to *Private Eye* was the most important part of his judgement.

A young *Sunday Times* reporter, Anthony Holden, however, aided and abetted by myself, had been following the case very closely. With the help of a colleague, Philip Knightley, he wrote a long account called 'The Mystery of the Two Missing Witnesses'. It appeared in the *Sunday Times* on 18 July.

This publicity had two immediate effects. On 19 July, immediately following publication of Donaldson's judgement, Leslie Paisner resigned. He gave ill health as his reason. One of his sons was quoted as saying: 'My father has been through a very harrowing experience.' Shortly afterwards, Paisner left for Israel, where he remained for several months.

Meanwhile, the publication of the *Sunday Times*'s article precipitated serious trouble for Addey. A PR man does not himself welcome the attention of the press. His job is to ensure favourable publicity for his clients, and this is best done by remaining in the background and, whenever possible, concealing the identity of his clients altogether. Thus, at a *Private Eye* lunch, for example, Addey would try to interest us in a story to the discredit of one of his client's rivals, without revealing who his client was. But the *Sunday Times* story focused attention on Addey himself and all his big clients. More than that, it showed him in a dubious light, firstly making a charge of blackmail against a journalist friend for no apparent reason, secondly fleeing to Italy when required to come to court.

The article sparked off a revolt in his boardroom which may well have been smouldering before the case. A week of meetings ended in the resignation of his Chairman, Sir Desmond Heap, and six of the directors on 12 August. At the same time, one of Addey's major clients, the big supermarket firm Tesco, announced that they were cancelling their PR contract with Addey, worth £10,000 pa. It was a tribute to Addey's continuing skill as a public relations man that this series of disasters was described in one paper as 'a triumph'.

The reverses suffered by the two men made me wonder yet again why they had both been prepared to sign statements which at the time they must have known could be ruinous to them, and which now had indeed proved to be so. Paisner had resigned in humiliating circumstances, Addey had lost half his directors and one of his most valuable clients; he was exposed as a homosexual, and was now facing a slander action for accusing a journalist in a sworn statement of a criminal offence.

The obvious implication was that some form of pressure had been exerted on them, and that both men were faced with alternatives which at the time made possible exposure seem preferable. What form the pressure took, we did not know. The only clue was Addey's remark that he had been threatened with a slander action. The same could well be true of Paisner, who could have been accused of slandering Levine to Addey and Marnham. But would that be enough to make an experienced old lawyer like Paisner sign his strange confession? The only other clue was Addey's remark to me , 'I did not realise they were so powerful.' What was that supposed to mean?

We did not know the answer. All the same, I decided that *Private Eye* ought, in everyone's interest, including Paisner's and Addey's, to set out the facts in as much detail as we could. Desmond Browne advised strongly against it. It was inviting a certain Contempt of Court case, he said. But, I argued, apart from the obvious importance of the story, it was vital to demonstrate to Goldsmith that we had not been gagged.

There was another point. In our researches into Goldsmith and Levine, two new stories had been unearthed. The first was that in 1975, just before Goldsmith took over as Chairman of Slater Walker, his Anglo-Continental company had been sued for 'fraudulent misrepresentation' by the merchant bankers Vavasseur, over the sale of a bank in Amsterdam. The second story concerned Levine's role in the affairs of the runaway MP John Stonehouse, who was at this time on trial at the Old Bailey on a variety of charges. Levine, we discovered, had been the legal adviser to Stonehouse's ramshackle bank, the British Bangladesh Trust, and it had been partly thanks to Levine's 'advice' that the bank had managed to survive for another year after its accounts had been queried by the auditors, Dixon Wilson, in 1973.

Both these stories were of considerable 'public interest'. Was *Private Eye* obliged to sit on them, therefore, while our libel actions ground slowly through the courts? If we did so, would we not be voluntarily submitting to the gag which Donaldson had refused to grant?

At the same time, the temptation to do nothing was a strong one. The strain of an apparently unending stream of cases was beginning to tell. I myself could talk or think of little but Goldsmith. At night I dreamed about him. The obsession was plainly turning me into a bore as far as my immediate circle was concerned, and meanwhile *Private Eye* was suffering from neglect. Could we afford the cost of another case?

In the end — rightly, I think — the spirit of 'once more into the breach' prevailed, and I decided to publish an account of the Donaldson case. Gillard and I thought it would be best written by someone not directly involved in the case, and so we asked Paul Foot if he would do it. Foot agreed, but after Desmond Browne had been to work on his initial draft, he would not have recognised it. Nothing was to be said to suggest that any particular individual brought pressure to bear on Addey and Paisner. The article, sticking closely to what people had said in their affidavits, would simply tell the story, culminating in the reverses suffered by the two men, and posing the question: why had they acted as they did? No article published in *Private Eye* has ever received such a thorough vetting beforehand. Desmond went over every word in every sentence with scrupulous care. The finished article, six columns long, was published under the heading 'The Erasing of Lazarus' on 28 August.

A week later, Goldsmith applied to the vacation judge to bring Contempt of Court proceedings.

Because of the lengthy legal vacation, the case was not due

to be heard until the end of October. It then came before the Lord Chief Justice, Lord Widgery, sitting with Mr Justice Eveleigh, who had presided over the marathon Stonehouse trial earlier in the year, and Mr Justice Peter Pain.

The law on Contempt of Court is extremely ill-defined, and is therefore much more of a headache to journalists than the law of libel. Its main purpose is to prevent the press or any other party from prejudicing a jury in advance of a trial, thereby jeopardising the chance of an accused man to be given a fair hearing. But, as we had seen with Lord Justice Salmon and the affair of the gagging writ, the law itself does not define the exact boundaries of contempt. In the absence of any clear rules, the judges are left to decide each case on its merits.

Hawser's argument was that 'The Erasing of Lazarus' — the headline itself, he said, was 'a very emotive phrase with Mafia connotations' — clearly suggested that Goldsmith and Levine had brought pressure to bear on Paisner and Addey, and that such a suggestion was in Contempt of Court. (If that indeed was what the piece suggested, it followed that it was highly libellous since to pressurise someone into signing a false statement is a criminal offence. Yet Goldsmith did not suggest at any time that the article was libellous.) Comyn replied that though I myself believed that pressure had been brought to bear — Addey, after all, had told me himself — the article did not say as much. It was only an inference that could be drawn, to the extent that a reader of the piece might ask, as Mr Justice Donaldson had done, 'Is the man mad? Or has someone twisted his arm?' (Widgery himself referred, less graphically, to 'the mystery as to whether they had been got at' and, if so, by whom?')

In this contempt hearing the *Eye* was assisted by two things. One was the *Sunday Times* article by Holden and Knightley, which had already covered some of the same ground. If the *Sunday Times* could write about the case, we argued, why not *Private Eye*? The other was simply the complexity of the story itself. The judges had to consider whether a potential juryman who read the article would be influenced, but it soon became clear that, to begin with at least, the Lord Chief Justice himself had difficulty in following the saga. After Hawser had been speaking for about an hour, introducing the various characters in the story — Goldsmith, Levine, Paisner, Addey, — Widgery interrupted him, saying: 'Mr Hawser, we've been listening to you for some time now. We've had many characters brought on the stage, colourfully painted by yourself. But I'm bound to say that I've still got very little idea of what all this is about.'

Once the judges did begin to grasp the story, however, it dawned on them that there were, after all, matters of some importance involved. As Mr Justice Peter Pain said to Hawser at one point: 'They [i.e. *Private Eye*] are bound to ask the question: what on earth persuaded Paisner and Addey to behave the way they did?' Pain also pointed out that by applying for the injunction and then bringing contempt proceedings Goldsmith was causing publicity to be given to the very matters which he was anxious should be suppressed.

This was indeed the case, and was, we assumed, an aspect of the affair that had not been welcomed by Mr Eric Levine. For, although Paisner's original allegations against him had never been published, the fact that Paisner had made allegations was now public knowledge. Inevitably, the spotlights were turned on Levine and it was plain that, being a man who, like Addey, preferred to operate behind the scenes, he did not relish the situation.

The hearing lasted for a week, and once again the length of the proceedings was attributable in part to the eloquence of Lewis Hawser, for there were no witnesses. At the end, the Lord Chief Justice was commendably brief. In contempt, he said, each case had to be decided on its merits. But in general, he added, ' . . . it seems to me that eventually one must decide by asking whether the action complained of does present a real risk that the fair trial of some particular legal proceedings in the future may be prejudiced.'

Hawser had argued that it did not matter whether proceed-

100

ings might be prejudiced. It was enough to show that someone had set out with the intention of prejudicing them, even if he had not, in fact, succeeded. But the recent case of Stephen Balogh, son of the Labour economist Lord Balogh, went against him. Balogh had been convicted of Contempt of Court for climbing on to the roof of St Albans Crown Court and trying to release laughing gas into the ventilation ducts, with the aim of livening up proceedings below. But Lord Denning, in the Appeal Court, ruled that as he had completely failed in this objective, there had been no contempt. The fact that he had intended to commit a Contempt of Court was not enough. Widgery therefore dismissed the application, and the other two judges agreed. Goldsmith was subsequently refused leave to appeal to the House of Lords.

The state of play was now as follows. Goldsmith had applied for an injunction to stop us writing about him and Levine; his application had been rejected by Mr Justice Donaldson. *Private Eye* had proceeded to write a long article about the case; Goldsmith had attempted to commit us to prison for Contempt of Court and had again failed.

Logically the next move was to print the other two stories, the Dutch bank, and Levine/Stonehouse, that had been put to one side pending the outcome of the Widgery hearing. But once again our lawyers advised against publication. We should be content, they said, with the Widgery victory. There were appeal cases in hand which further attacks on Goldsmith could jeopardise. I agreed at least to get these out of the way first.

Eventually, however, *Private Eye* published both stories, again after the most careful vetting — Levine/Stonehouse on 21 January 1977, and the Dutch bank on 18 February.

There was no reaction from Goldsmith or Levine on either occasion.

A Setback

All through the Goldsmith case there was a lot of talk in the papers and elsewhere about the freedom of the press. This talk concentrated on the issue of Criminal Libel. The resurrection of the old law, with its penalty of imprisonment seemed to many to pose a threat. And yet, paradoxically, by activating the law, Goldsmith provoked a furore which could well lead to its abolition.

At the same time, the irony was that, from an editor's point of view, the sanctions of Criminal Libel seemed in some ways preferable to those of the civil law. At the worst, I could be sent to prison; according to James Comyn, however, a fine was more likely. But in 1976 three plaintiffs in libel actions — Telly Savalas, Lord Bernstein and Mr Robin Herbert, Deputy Chairman of the Countryside Commission, were awarded damages of over £30,000 by juries for libels infinitely less serious than anything we had said about Goldsmith. Indeed the following year the editor of the homosexual paper *Gay News* was fined a mere £500 for printing a 'blasphemous libel'.

By suing the *Private Eye* distributors, however, Goldsmith did seriously threaten the freedom of the press in a quite unprecedented way, and one which, in the long run, was approved by the law at its highest level.

Private Eye had always been aware that distributors were liable to be sued. It was for that reason that the two biggest wholesale distributors in the United Kingdom, W.H. Smith and John Menzies, had refused from the beginning to sell *Private Eye*. They argued that people who did not sue the magazine on the grounds that we had no money would go after them instead.

This presumably was the idea behind the law; to give a plaintiff a remedy against a paper without any financial backing. If the editor and publisher had no assets, he could hope to recoup some damages from the printer and distributor. But, according to the legal textbooks, the latter can defend himself by pleading 'innocent dissemination'; that is, he can claim (a) that he did not know that the book or paper contained the libel complained of, or (b) that he did not know the book or paper was of a character likely to contain a libel.

It was on this issue of distributors' liability that Paul Foot and I had given evidence to the Faulks Committee in 1974. We argued that the law gave distributors an excuse to operate what amounted to censorship, pointing out that as a result of the ban by Smiths and Menzies *Private Eye* was deprived of a huge potential sale. But our points were summarily dismissed in the report. As with Criminal Libel, the committee, which was obviously dominated by its lawyer members, upheld the *status quo*.

The sale of any magazine is normally handled by one firm of distributors, which in turn parcels out copies either directly to retailers or to other wholesalers, each 'middle-man' taking a percentage of the cover price. Normally, when someone issues a writ, he sues the publisher, printer and the main distributor. The publisher, however, has nearly always indemnified his printer and distributor against having to pay any damages, and they are therefore only liable if the publisher goes bankrupt.

However, when Goldsmith sued, he sued not only our main distributor, Moore-Harness Ltd, but thirty-seven secondary wholesalers and retailers as well. The victims were evidently chosen hurriedly and at random, for they included three firms that did not sell *Private Eye* at all, and one that had recently been taken over by Cavenham.

They were sued for distributing not the issue containing the alleged Criminal Libel (the Elwes issue), but the two subsequent libels, Slater Walker and Levine. The reason for this became clear later.

The issuing of the writs caused some consternation in the trade, as most of the firms had no experience of such litigation. To begin with there was something of a panic, and one firm, Edward Martin, even decided there and then, on receipt of the writ, to discontinue the sale of *Private Eye*.

To the others Levine made it clear that Goldsmith was not interested in damages. If they would give an assurance never to sell *Private Eye* again, he would drop his actions. Some agreed to this deal without further ado. Others, however, demurred, and offered more limited undertakings, for example that they would suspend sales until the dispute had been resolved one way or the other in the courts.

But Levine made it clear that such agreements were not good enough. The solicitors of those firms who dithered were sent a uniform warning:

> 'We have not, thus far, issued proceedings against your clients in connection with the article published on page sixteen of the 12th December 1975 issue of *Private Eye* [the Elwes article]. This is because our client takes so serious a view of the defamatory nature of the article that, on the advice of leading counsel, we have applied for leave to commence Criminal Libel proceedings against the editor, proprietor and principal distributors in respect of it. We do however feel it only fair that your clients should be warned that our client fully reserves his rights against your clients in respect of their distribution of this defamatory article.'

The obvious implication of this letter of Levine's was a threat of Criminal Libel proceedings against the firms concerned unless they came to heel.

In the end — discounting the four rogue distributors — sixteen out of the thirty-seven agreed to Goldsmith's terms. The remaining seventeen decided to continue selling *Private Eye* and to defend the actions. Advised by Peter Bowsher, then acting as our junior counsel, we applied on behalf of the seventeen to have all the actions dismissed, or stayed, on the grounds that, under the Judicature Act of 1925, they were 'frivolous, vexatious and/or an abuse of the process of the court'.

The main argument in support of this claim was that, by suing the minor distributors and settling with them on the terms agreed, Goldsmith's aim was not to obtain the legitimate redress guaranteed him by the law, i.e. damages or an injunction, but rather the shutting-off of the *Eye*'s distribution channels and thus possibly its eventual demise.

The move had at least one beneficial result. If Goldsmith was considering any more writs against distributors, he did not issue them — though in principal there was nothing to stop him going after every single one of them and reducing the *Eye*'s circulation — already down by 12,000 — even more.

In the courts, too, we began with a success. On 26 June, Master Warren, convinced by Michael Kempster's arguments, ruled that the actions should be stayed. But Goldsmith, inevitably, appealed, and that October, in a higher court, Mr Justice Stocker ruled in his favour, arguing that in suing the distributors it was not Goldsmith's sole motive to cut off the sales outlets. He did not, he said, see any threat to the freedom of the press; and anyway, if there was one, it was a matter for Parliament to remedy.

To the reader who has followed this story through its earlier dramas, this may seem a minor and rather dull issue. But to us at *Private Eye*, as to many others at the time, it seemed an important point, perhaps the most important of all from a legal point of view. Here, we felt, was a genuine new threat to the freedom of the press, and one which could affect us disastrously in future. We also felt a strong obligation towards these distribution firms, many of them small, who had supported us so loyally over the years.

We therefore decided to take the case to the Court of Appeal, where it would almost certainly be heard by Lord Denning.

Since his appointment as Master of the Rolls in 1962, Lord Denning has gained a reputation among journalists as a judge who, unlike almost all his fellows, does really believe in the freedom of the press. Time and again, in cases involving newspapers, Denning had overruled the decisions of lower courts to the advantage of newspapers. Such an attitude in a British judge is extremely rare. Our judges, on the whole, regard the press as a nuisance and in some cases as a threat to their own authority. Denning takes a more 'American' view, giving precedence to press freedom over the power of other litigants.

In December 1976, when our distributors appeal came before him, Denning was seventy-seven. He had, to the annoyance of some colleagues, escaped a recent rule making it compulsory for judges to retire at the age of seventy-five. Ruddy-faced, wearing a short wig, peering out into court with his head cupped in his left hand, Denning looked and spoke like an old Hampshire farmer. His pleasant rustic voice struck a delightfully incongruous note in the heavy courtroom atmosphere.

Denning was the only judge in the course of the Goldsmith case who was wholeheartedly on *Private Eye*'s side. In this he seemed to follow the old Tory establishment, like Lord Crathorne, head of the Honours Scrutiny Committee, who had said of the controversial lords and knights: 'We didn't like the cut of their jib.' Whereas Judge Wien, for example, had taken the view that Goldsmith was a pillar of society, Denning's remarks throughout implied that he did not think so much either of him or his lawyer Levine. The key word in his vocabulary was 'respectable'. The distributors were all respectable firms — wholesalers and retailers 'of good standing'. The *Observer*, to which he referred in passing, was 'a highly respectable paper'. Goldsmith and Levine were not so described.

I had been told before the case that Denning was not popular with his fellow lawyers because he refused to 'go by the book'.

He preferred to make his own law in the interests of justice and common sense. So it was here. Everyone assumed that the distributors were liable to be sued; the question was whether Goldsmith was entitled to use the legal process for the secondary purpose of shutting off the channels of distribution. But Denning, with unfaultable logic, questioned the basic assumption that a distributor could be sued, except in exceptional circumstances. Take a paper like the *Observer*, he said:

'Bundles of it come in and go out very quickly. The distributors have no opportunity to read all the articles in it; and if they did, they have no chance of enquiring whether the facts are true or the comment fair . . . . Common sense and fairness require that no subordinate distributor — from top to bottom — should be held liable for a libel contained in it unless he knew or ought to have known that the newspaper or periodical contained a libel on the plaintiff himself that could not be justified or excused; and I should have thought that it was for the plaintiff to prove this . . .

[So much for the 'respectable' paper.] But what about publications which are contentious and controversial such as *Private Eye*? It is said that a publication may have so bad a character — and be so likely to contain a libel — that anyone who distributes it knowing of its character, is liable for damages to any person who is libelled in it . . . I suppose there may be some publications which are so bad — so prone to libel without just cause or excuse — that no distributor should handle them; or at any rate should handle them at his peril. But there would have to be very strong evidence before it reached that point. Even though a publication may be contentious or controversial — even though it may be scurrilous and give offence to many — it is not to be banned on that account. After all, who is to be the censor? Who is to assess its worth? Who is to enquire how many libel writs have been issued against it? And whether the words were true or the comment fair? No distributor can be expected to do it. Nor, later on, can a jury.'

Denning made one other obvious point. Where was the liability to end? If the law was applied:

> 'It would mean that all the firms who distribute *Private Eye*, from the top to the bottom; all the bookstalls who sell it; all the public libraries who stock it; all the clubs and common rooms who take it — and there are many who do — and everyone who hands it to his neighbour to read — each and every one of them would be liable in damages to any person — to any member of the public at large — who claims that he has been libelled in it.'

It is worth quoting Lord Denning at some length, not only because of the good sense of his conclusions, but because, unlike the utterances of most judges, they are perfectly intelligible. Normally, when a lawyer begins to speak, the ordinary man switches off after a few minutes, finding it impossible to follow what the man is talking about, or, if he can, realising that it has little bearing on reality. Denning spoke simply and directly, and for the first time during the case, I had a sense of the law as a living thing rather than something buried in a pile of dusty tomes.

It was, I suppose, too much to expect that his view would be shared by the other two judges, Lord Justices Scarman and Bridge, even though the former had the reputation of being a 'liberal'. Scarman, who spoke next, had soon embarked on the traditional legal gobbledygook: 'The plaintiff's purpose has to be shown to be not that which the law by granting a remedy offers to fulfil but one which the law does not recognise as a legitimate use of the remedy sought, see Re Majory (1955) I Chancery at page 623', etc.

Both these other two judges agreed with Justice Stocker that if there was any threat to press freedom, then it was up to Parliament to change the law. Lord Justice Bridge, whose hostility to *Private Eye* had been obvious from the start, even ticked Denning off for the way he had summed up: 'There is a breach of the rule *audi alteram partem* which applies alike to issues of law, as to issues of fact, and in a court of inferior jurisdiction this would be a ground for *certiorari . . .'*

Denning had been overruled by two to one, and *Private Eye* was refused leave to appeal to the House of Lords.

Biggles to the Rescue

The attempt to get Goldsmith's actions against the distributors dismissed had failed. Logically, the next step was for the distributors to go to court and fight the libel actions along with us.

But was this sensible or even plausible? The *Eye's* defeat had had two effects. One was financial. The hearing, which had lasted for a whole week, instead of the two days which had been expected, meant another huge bill for legal costs. In December 1976, the Goldenballs Fund stood at £36,000, boosted by the recent addition of £6,000 from an auction of paintings and manuscripts organised by Tony Rushton. But it looked as if this was not going to be nearly enough to go on fighting, even with transfusions from the *Eye's* own profits.

The second effect was psychological. We had now fought one battle in the campaign all the way through the courts, the battle in which *Private Eye* seemed to have right on its side more than in any other, and despite Lord Denning's magnificent judgement, we had lost the case. The outcome reinforced my natural disillusionment with the legal system and my conviction that, although we had won a double victory on the Contempt of Court issue, it was vain to look to the law for any vindication.

The affair had been going on for over a year and had involved at least a dozen court hearings. But now most of the issues had been decided one way or the other. Ahead of us lay only the Criminal Libel case, which had been set down to be heard on 10 May. This was to be the grand finale at the Old Bailey, but it had been deferred for so long and so many other cases had intervened that I had almost forgotten about it. Even now there was something a little unreal about being charged with a criminal offence for having written something. The idea of being sent to prison for it seemed even more remote.

Yet, as the case loomed up, the possibility had to be considered. I had seen enough of the unpredictability of judges to be prepared for anything. Our case was very weak. We had already acknowledged that the article was libellous. Our only hope lay in another display of hysterics from Goldsmith and the purely legal argument that to justify a criminal interpretation there had to be a breach of the peace. This would probably entail an appeal to the House of Lords. All in all, therefore, the future looked bleak.

In the meantime, Goldsmith was busy with a new interest. With Wilson's retirement, his hopes of a political career were dashed. Now, it seemed, he had developed ambitions of being a press lord, partly because it offered the next best thing — Stanley Baldwin's 'power without responsibility' — but also because his experiences with *Private Eye* had left him with the conviction that what he lacked was a 'platform' from which to broadcast his point of view. To a man like Goldsmith, the best way to getting a platform was to buy one.

1976 was a good time to come shopping in Fleet Street. The whole industry was in a state of chaos. As the pound fell, the price of paper was rising all the time; over-manning was still as rife as ever, and the patience of the hereditary press lords, some of whom kept papers in business mainly for personal prestige, was running out.

The future of certain papers, owned by an industrial conglomerate which could support a loss-making newspaper with profits from other businesses, seemed reasonably assured. But others without such support were much more vulnerable to sudden crises. The *Observer* had been in difficulties for some time and its proprietor, David Astor, who had edited the paper for nearly thirty years, was increasingly wearied by interminable disputes with the printing unions. His decision to compete directly with the expanding *Sunday Times* had proved a costly failure. At the end of 1975 he gave up his editorship at the age of sixty-three, to be succeeded by Donald Trelford. Astor seemed reluctant to relinquish complete control, and he remained the principal shareholder. Despite economies, however, the paper's position worsened, and in the autumn of 1976 Astor approached the government for help. It was not forthcoming. Unwilling and unable to sacrifice the interests of his family by altering the terms of the trust which controlled the newspaper, he decided to sell it, and, with the Chairman of the trustees, Lord Goodman, began to look around for a suitable buyer.

Surprisingly, in view of the paper's precarious state, several parties seemed interested. They included Associated Newspapers, owners of the *Daily Mail*, who lacked a Sunday newspaper; Rupert Murdoch, favoured by Goodman, proprietor of the *Sun* and *News of the World*, and thought to be eager to acquire a serious paper to improve his image; a Hong Kong publishing group headed by Miss Sally Law Sian; Olga Deterding, the oil heiress; a mysterious Arab consortium; and Sir James Goldsmith. One by one, the others dropped out, leaving the field at the beginning of November to Harmsworth (*of the Mail*) and Goldsmith.

At his Anglo-Continental offices in Leadenhall Street, Goldsmith, employing all his powers to charm, played host to delegations of journalists and printers, who, if reports were to be believed, had a considerable say in deciding who the new owner of the newspaper would be. Even quite experienced journalists were impressed by him. He was not, he stressed, a right-wing extremist. He would call himself a man of the centre. At the same time, he denied he would ever force his views into the paper against the wishes of the editorial staff. Everyone was reassured.

But Goldsmith found himself up against one bulky obstacle in the shape of Lord Goodman, Chairman of the *Observer* Trust, and also at the time Chairman of the Newspaper Publishers'

Association. It soon became clear that Goodman had taken a most vehement dislike to Goldsmith. 'He would rather go on a diet than do a deal with him', one government minister was quoted as saying, and to the *Observer* journalists Goodman went even further, maintaining at one point that in his view it would be better for the paper to fold altogether rather than end up in Goldsmith's possession.

This strong antipathy on Goodman's part was not new. It was widely believed that it had been Goodman who had leaked the story of the Goldsmith honour to the press, hoping presumably to promote a campaign which would put paid to it. But, unlike many of those who came out most strongly against Goldsmith, his hostility towards the man had nothing to do with *Private Eye*, a magazine which Goodman, as one of its oldest butts, had good cause to detest. Goodman had knowledge of Goldsmith from two sources. One of his closest friends and associates was the property developer Lord Rayne, like Goodman an active patron of the arts and a keen Zionist. Rayne was married to Annabel Birley's sister, Jane. The Raynes resented the fact that Goldsmith showed no inclination to divorce his wife and marry Lady Annabel. Goodman also had professional knowledge of Goldsmith. He had been involved with him on at least two occasions. Goodman had been called in to mediate in the embarrassing affair of the Dutch Bank in 1975, when Goldsmith's Anglo-Continental was being sued for 'fraudulent misrepresentation'. He had found against Goldsmith. He had also travelled with Goldsmith to Singapore in an attempt to settle the dispute between Slater Walker and Haw Par. He therefore had first-hand experience of Goldsmith's business methods.

Goodman's opposition played a vital role in blocking Goldsmith's hopes of acquiring the *Observer*, which was finally sold to a last-minute bidder, the American oil company, Atlantic Richfield. But Goldsmith had discovered, too, during his discussions with journalists, that his continuing litigation with *Private Eye* was considered a black mark against him. It was not

113

perhaps surprising that *Observer* journalists, faced with the possible closure of their newspaper, should be animated by the principle of 'any port in a storm'; none of them made any attempt to enquire into the details of the *Private Eye* dispute. They were, however, sufficiently alert to realise that it would look bad for a paper with a long tradition of liberalism to sell itself to someone who was at that point trying to put an editor in prison and stop his paper being sold by its distributors.

It was perhaps because of this that during the *Observer* negotiations Goldsmith made another attempt at a settlement. I myself had already offered, while the contempt case was in progress before Lord Widgery, to settle on the basis of an apology and a payment of £20,000 towards his costs. Goldsmith now seemed eager to take me up on this, but, as often happens, once the lawyers got together to fix the details, a number of snags arose. (Hawser was plainly just as keen as Goldsmith not to lose face.) Once again, Goldsmith tried to gain, in addition, an undertaking which would have restricted our freedom to write about him. He was unwilling, too, to settle his slander action with Gillard as part of a general amnesty. The settlement talks broke down.

The *Observer* was sold to the Americans. The Court of Appeal sided with Goldsmith in the distributors' case. Meanwhile, by April 1977, another newspaper seemed to be in the death-throes. Like the *Observer*, Beaverbrook Newspapers, publishers of the *Daily Express* and its stablemates the *Evening Standard* and the *Sunday Express*, had no wealthy subsidiaries to help support it. Although the *Sunday Express* was profitable, the *Daily Express* was losing money heavily. Under a series of uninspiring editors, the circulation had fallen from 3.4 million in 1971 to 2.5 million in 1976. Like David Astor, the proprietor — Sir Max Aitken — nicknamed 'Biggles' by *Private Eye* — who had never shared his father's interest in newspapers, was losing heart. His health was failing and he had sustained a series of strokes. In April 1977, he resumed talks with his old rivals, Associated Newspapers, owners of the *Daily Mail*, about a plan to sell them the *Evening Standard*, which would then be merged with Associated's *Evening News*. The story was leaked to the press, an angry reaction ensued at the *Standard*, and Goldsmith, who already owned thirty-five per cent of Beaverbrook's non-voting shares, once again stepped forward with an offer to salvage the paper. As before, delegations of the NUJ, led by the paper's newly-appointed young editor, Simon Jenkins, trotted round to Leadenhall Street to hear him outline his plans for their possible survival.

On 5 May, eleven days before the Criminal Libel case was due to begin at the Old Bailey, I had arranged to have lunch with Jenkins, hoping to get some information about the *Standard* story for *Private Eye*. Jenkins, however, showed no inclination to talk about that, nor did he seem very interested in my views on Goldsmith's suitablility to become the owner of a newspaper. What he wanted to know was whether I was prepared to settle with Goldsmith. I said I had always been in favour of an amnesty, so long as the terms were right. Jenkins said that he had already spoken to Goldsmith and that he was willing to deploy what he called 'maximum flexibility'. It was obvious that, once again, as with the *Observer*, the continuing *Eye* litigation was hampering Goldsmith's ambitions of becoming a press lord, and now, in addition, the prospect of having to sit in court for up to two weeks while the Criminal Libel case ground on was, of course, very inconvenient.

That same afternoon, following a meeting with Goldsmith, Jenkins met me in a Soho coffee bar to tell me the terms: an apology to be published as a full-page advertisement in the *Evening Standard* — Jenkins assured me we would get it at a bargain rate — and a contribution towards Goldsmith's costs of £30,000, payable over ten years. The *Eye*'s distributors would be released from their undertakings. There was no mention of Levine, and the Gillard slander action remained outstanding. Without waiting to consult my lawyers, I agreed. It seemed that the situation at the *Standard* was so fluid that Goldsmith's attitude could easily change overnight, especially if we began to haggle.

There had been some doubt as to whether it was possible to stop the Criminal Libel case once the Crown had taken over the prosecution. But eventually the lawyers had agreed among themselves that it could be done. It still meant, however, that on the appointed day, 16 May, Marnham and myself had to enter the dock at the Old Bailey's famous Number One Court and plead 'Not Guilty' to the charge of Criminal Libel. Lewis Hawser then rose and explained to the judge, Mr Justice Bristow, that *Private Eye* had apologised to Sir James in an advertisement in the *Evening Standard*, which he then read out:

> 'During the past few months much publicity has been given to the litigation between Sir James Goldsmith and *Private Eye*.
>
> The history of the matter began in December 1975, when *Private Eye* published an article which referred to the Lucan affair. It was that article which became the subject of Sir James's widely-publicised Criminal Libel proceedings in respect of that article and three later articles on different subjects. Since then, there has been further litigation about whether *Private Eye* had published, or was about to publish, articles in Contempt of Court.
>
> *Private Eye* now recognises that any suggestion in the issue of 12th December 1975 that Sir James had taken part in a criminal conspiracy was particularly serious, and wishes to make it known publicly once and for all that there was not a shred of truth in it.
>
> *Private Eye* accepts that Sir James would have been entitled to very substantial damages for what *Private Eye* said about him. He has, however, made it clear that our unreserved apology will satisfy him and he has waived his rights to damages.
>
> Some readers may remember that in the summer of last year Richard Ingrams was interviewed on the BBC

116

television programme, *The Editors*. He stated that *Private Eye* would sometimes publish apologies or retractions not because what it had originally published was untrue but because *Private Eye* did not have the resources to prove it in court.

Private Eye wishes to make it absolutely clear that this is not such a case, and genuinely and unreservedly apologises to Sir James. In proof of that *Private Eye* has agreed to pay Sir James a substantial contribution towards his legal costs.

It has never been the intention of *Private Eye* to pursue any personal or public vendetta against Sir James Goldsmith and he has our assurance that we will not do so in future issues of *Private Eye*.'

Marnham and I were then pronounced 'Not Guilty'.

I left the dock with the strong conviction that we would have lost the case. The atmosphere of the criminal court was especially forbidding, and Mr Justice Bristow had been the judge who, a few months before, had given Mrs Whitehouse leave to bring a prosecution against *Gay News* for blasphemous libel. This was not in any way to belittle the powers as an advocate of James Comyn, who had acted throughout with exceptional shrewdness. He himself, however, had always been pessimistic about our chances in the criminal case.

There was a small school of die-hards who said that I should have fought on regardless. But it was difficult to see what purpose would have been served, except to make a martyr of myself and perhaps to force the House of Lords to redefine the law of Criminal Libel. It was a pity to leave this issue unresolved, but after the distributors' case I reposed no great faith in the legal system as champion of press freedom, and *Private Eye* had better things to do than to play the part of legal guinea-pig. Besides, there would have been additional expense on a huge scale. The readers had by now contributed over £40,000 to the defence fund and we could hardly go on indefinitely asking them to subsidise what some of them, with justification, might interpret as an obsession. Already, after thirteen court hearings of one sort or another, most people had lost the thread of the story.

As it happened, however, the debate about Criminal Libel was not allowed to die. A few weeks after the settlement, one Roger Gleaves, who had just served part of a four-year sentence for sexual and other offences against young boys, sued Yorkshire Television for Criminal Libel in relation to a documentary about male prostitution called *Johnny Go Home* in which he had featured. In the course of legal researches in prison, Gleaves had discovered that the Criminal Libel law was so infrequently used that it had never been amended to cover television. Although it was necessary when suing a newspaper to first seek leave from a High Court judge, no such rule applied as far as TV was concerned.

The case came up before Mrs Audrey Frisby, stipendiary magistrate at Wells Street Court, London, in September 1976. Understandably in the circumstances, counsel for Yorkshire television argued that Gleaves, a convicted criminal, should not be allowed to institute criminal proceedings. Mrs Frisby, however, took the view that if a man of 'impeccable reputation' like Sir James Goldsmith was allowed to sue for Criminal Libel, then there was no reason why a man in Gleaves's position should not be given the same privilege. Such a man, she argued, might well not be able to afford a civil action.

At the time of writing, this case has yet to be resolved. It could well be, however, that Mrs Frisby, whether intentionally or not, has thrown a spanner in the works which will force the legal establishment to decide whether they really want to retain the law of Criminal Libel.*

The important victory that *Private Eye* had won, and which was not in any way jeopardised by the settlement, was to establish our freedom to write about Goldsmith. He was, and still is, free to sue *Private Eye* at any time, but in the end he did accept that he could not control what we said about him, or about Eric Levine for that matter, in advance of publication.

For Goldsmith personally the settlement was obviously a big climb-down and, as often happened on such occasions, he was plunged into gloom. His spirits cannot have improved when, after all, he failed to gain control of the *Daily Express* group, which was sold a week or two later to Trafalgar House, owners of the Cunard Shipping Company.

After months of living with Goldsmith, I found it hard to believe that the whole thing was over and that I had at last got him off my back. It was only when I read the *Sunday Telegraph* on 15 May that I felt reassured. 'As far as I am concerned,' Goldsmith told Ivan Rowan, very coldly, *'Private Eye* is past history.'

*Eventually, the case reached the House of Lords, which confirmed that the 'breach of the peace' criterion is not an essential ingredient for leave to bring a Criminal Libel action. What matters is that the libel is 'serious' rather than 'trivial', though little guidance was given on what makes a trivial libel serious. Mr Justice Taylor, in the 1982 case *Desmond v Thorne* said he thought it undesirable to lay down detailed criteria and that it was better for judges to have a wide measure of discretion in deciding whether to grant leave to bring proceedings. From a litigant's point of view, the law remains as unclear as ever.

Who Done It?

In real life there are few clear-cut victories, in the courts or elsewhere. Nor can stories come to an end with their mysteries all neatly resolved. This book began with one of the best known and most intriguing mysteries of recent years, that of Lord Lucan. Is he alive or dead? The question remains, to our annoyance, unanswered. After my personal researches I can only say that either he is alive, or, if he is dead, that his body was concealed or destroyed by accomplices in order to save his children, particularly, from the disgrace of what could be interpreted as a clear admission of guilt. What is most probable is that he committed suicide in such a way as to conceal his body, for example by loading himself with weights and jumping into the sea.

The whole Clermont tradition, however, which makes every situation into a gamble, presupposes me to think that he is still alive. (It is worth noting, however, that at the famous lunch party, Aspinall, who has something of an obsession with suicide, said that Lucan should choose the Roman way out, and 'die on his own sword.')

One or two of the riddles were eventually solved — for example the mysterious gift of £5,000 from 'Tiny' Rowland. It appears that some time towards the end of 1974 Goldsmith, along with Jim Slater and Roland Franklin, bet Rowland £10,000 that Edward Heath, who had just lost the second of that year's general elections, would be back in power by the end of 1975. The deadline passed and, far from being Prime Minister, Heath was voted out of the Tory leadership and replaced by Margaret

Thatcher. Rowland asked for his money. Slater and Franklin, both of whom had by then fallen on hard times, pleaded poverty, leaving Goldsmith to pay up. By April 1976, when the Wien hearing took place, Rowland had still not received the £10,000 due to him. He decided to give £5,000 to *Private Eye*. Goldsmith remonstrated, and was told that we would get another £5,000 unless he paid up at once. He did so.

Other, more relevant, mysteries remain. Why was Goldsmith so anxious to defend Levine, even to the extent, in my own view, of throwing away his commanding position in the *Private Eye* litigation? He went to such exaggerated lengths to protect him that in the end Levine became a marked man, and his name was picked up by the press in December 1977 when the Department of Trade report into Stonehouse's bank was published, severely reprimanding both him and the bank's accountant, Sir Charles Hardie.

Goldsmith's friends spoke frequently of his loyalty, a minor virtue much extolled at the Clermont Club. 'The one thing I loathe most of all,' said Goldsmith himself, when asked about Joe Haines's book on Wilson, 'are traitors.' Elwes, like Haines, was a traitor in the eyes of the Clermont set; and at Bow Street Goldsmith went out of his way to make a ringing declaration of his devotion to Lucan. Was it then loyalty alone that spurred him on to protect his lawyer? We do not know.

The behaviour of Addey and Paisner likewise has yet to be explained. If anything, in view of the recent settlement of Gillard's slander action against Addey, the mystery has deepened. Addey, at last, in a statement in Open Court made on October 1978, withdrew the charge of blackmail and agreed to pay Gillard £5,000 to compensate him. But he did not explain how he came to make an allegation which he later acknowledged to be completely false. Despite this complete retraction, in June 1979 Goldsmith contested the slander action brought by Gillard and surprisingly won the case. Goldsmith, who never denied spreading the story round Fleet Street, maintained that Addey's apology was insincere, that Gillard was a blackmailer and the *Eye* a magazine 'steeped in blackmail'. Though Addey, once again, did not give evidence, the jury accepted the Goldsmith version of events.

As for Paisner, he later confided in a friend that he had signed his 'confession' without even reading it. He also suggested that as a devout Jew his concern at the time had been to protect the good name of the Jewish community by preventing unsavoury disclosures about his firm, whose many important Jewish clients included Sir Isaac Wolfson, President of the United Synagogue — a position second only in importance to that of Chief Rabbi. But that was as far as he would go. In an attempt to get to the bottom of the affair, I asked the Law Society in December 1976 to investigate the circumstances in which he signed his affidavit. In March 1978, the Society reported that they had adjourned their enquiry *sine die* and declined to give a reason for their decision. Paisner died on 28 March 1979.

Two other questions remain. Why did Goldsmith issue such an extraordinary barrage of writs against *Private Eye* and its distributors? And why, above all, was he nominated for a peerage in Harold Wilson's Honours List? After many months of puzzlement I came in the end to the conclusion that there was one answer to both questions.

After making allowances for Goldsmith's fierce hostility to adverse criticism, our first feeling, as I have described, about the scale of the litigation was that there might be some terrible skeleton in his cupboard, publication of which he was determined to forestall. But as we dug deeper and deeper into his cupboard, no obvious bones came to light.

The peerage was even more puzzling, for on the surface Goldsmith had done nothing whatever for Wilson, apart from meeting him on a few occasions and giving him advice on French methods of economic planning. But suppose the two things were connected. Suppose, in other words, that Goldsmith was honoured partly for the very reason that he had sued *Private Eye* . . . .

Such a theory appears perhaps at first sight fanciful, unless one bears in mind from the start that, despite her denials, the notorious Honours List was the work of the capricious Lady Falkender and that the names on it were her names, not Wilson's. More than anything, Falkender used the list as a last chance to reward friends and pay off old scores, and they, like Wilson to a lesser extent, had an obsession about *Private Eye*.

There were, for a start, our constant references to Wilson's band of cronies and supporters, the East/West traders like Kagan, Rudy Sternberg and Montague Meyer. (Wilson himself had even issued a writ when, in 1971, Auberon Waugh jokingly referred to the fact that Kagan had employed him as a male model in order to sell his Gannex mackintoshes.) But the final act of treachery on our part came in 1974 when, in the wake of revelations about Marcia's involvement with her brother in land speculation — the so-called 'Slagheap Affair' — *Private Eye*, in the course of a long article about her, revealed for the first time the existence of her two illegitimate children by the *Daily Mail*'s political correspondent, Walter Terry. Although this was a story that was well known in Fleet Street, no paper had published it before. Our article caused a tremendous rumpus. Falkender herself later wrote that there had once been an occasion when she had been so outraged by something that *Private Eye* had said about her that she had to be restrained from coming round to Greek Street and punching me in the face.

In any case, as the *Private Eye*/Goldsmith case went on, it became clear that Wilson and Falkender were actively involved on the Goldsmith side. 'Equally remarkable', Michael Davie had written in the *Observer* on 19 May 1976, 'he [Goldsmith] has been getting advice about his *Private Eye* problems from none other than Sir Harold Wilson.' Davie also referred to the fact that at one time there had been talk of Goldsmith setting up a £250,000 fund to which anyone who considered himself libelled by *Private Eye* could apply for legal aid. Nothing came of this, though it is conceivably relevant that the only other person to threaten Criminal Libel proceedinsg against the *Eye* in the wake of Goldsmith was another friend of Falkender's, Jeremy

Thorpe, who also complained in a lawyer's letter about a 'campaign of vilification'. (Thorpe never acted on his threat, once the matter was publicised.)

Wilson cropped up in the story on at least two subsequent occasions, firstly offering newspapers a list of *Private Eye* informers, a list that could only have been compiled with the help of Goldsmith's 'highly reputable' firm of dustbin scavengers, and secondly passing on the story of Gillard's alleged blackmailing of Addey to the editor of the *Observer*, Donald Trelford. Marcia's greatest friend and ally, the publisher George Weidenfeld, was also involved in spreading the story.

There were other indications of a common cause. All these people — Goldsmith, Wilson, Weidenfeld and Falkender — used in public the same justification for their hostility to *Private Eye*, namely that it was 'anti-Semitic'. Another Falkender ally, David Frost, made the same charge. Goldsmith told several journalists, including Anthony Lewis of the *New York Times*, that it was for this reason that he had proceeded against us — a curious crusade for someone who was only slightly Jewish, and without any overt Zionist associations, to embark on. (In fact, I would maintain that *Private Eye* is no more anti-Semitic than it is anti-anything, but both Wilson and Falkender were sensitive to the fact that almost all the men on the Honours List were Jews, despite the unnecessary scrupulousness of the press in not referring to it. The truth is, perhaps, that the charge of anti-Semitism provided a convenient, and unanswerable, attack to critics of the list.)

Goldsmith himself later used another justification for his campaign, namely that *Private Eye* was anti-democratic. Coming from someone who had constantly deplored the democratic process as inefficient and unworkable, this seemed a little odd. But, again, it was a charge that Wilson himself made. Relying on the, by this time, rather tenuous connection between *Private Eye* and Paul Foot, a leading member of the Socialist Workers Party, Wilson argued that *Private Eye* was a quasi-revolutionary organ dedicated to the overthrow of the system by discrediting social-democrat politicians like himself. Goldsmith developed this theme with many vivid pathological analogies: *Private Eye* was a 'pus seeping through the system', a cancer gnawing away at the heart of the British way of life.

Later I received from two sources confirmation of my theory that the peerage and the *Eye* litigation were connected. In December 1976 I was told by Peter Jay, who had heard it himself from David Frost, that at their very first meeting at Frost's house in July 1975, Goldsmith had discussed *Private Eye* with Wilson and Falkender, and had there and then offered to rid them of 'this turbulent magazine'. At that time, of course, Goldsmith had no real axe to grind against the *Eye*, though it may have been at this stage that the £250,000 fund was mooted. As luck would have it, a few months later *Private Eye* played into Goldsmith's hands by publishing three pieces about him, thereby giving him an ideal opportunity to vindicate his reputation and at the same time endear himself to Wilson and Falkender.

This view of things was confirmed from another source, namely the *Evening Standard* journalist Sam White, who is an old friend of Goldsmith's. I met White by chance early in 1978 at the house of a mutual friend. Without any prompting from me, he stated that after recent conversations with him, he was sure that the reason Goldsmith was honoured was because he had sued *Private Eye*. The honour, he said, was intended both as a reward and to give him a higher standing with judge and jury when the case came to court.

White added one fascinating and, to me, clinching proof of this version of events.

Goldsmith's citation in the Honours List — 'for services to exports and ecology' — was the subject of much ridicule at the time the list was published. Goldsmith, after all, was not an exporter, and it was his brother Teddy who was the ecologist. Here was proof of the cynicism that lay behind the awards, it was said. But amid the general derision no one looked for a possible explanation of this curious phrase — 'for services to exports and ecology'. If, as everyone assumed, it was a mere cipher, why had they not put something that accorded with the facts — 'for services to the retail trade', for example? It was Sam White who pointed out to me that in fact the citation was a private joke between Goldsmith, Wilson and Falkender. Goldsmith's 'services to ecology', he said, consisted of ridding the country of the pollution of *Private Eye*.

I am convinced that this is the only possible explanation of the mysterious citation. (The reference to exports remains a mystery.) It is exactly the kind of joke which would appeal to Falkender and Goldsmith.

Ironically, though, the joke misfired completely, and the pollution which Goldsmith was to have destroyed only got worse. By suing in such an exaggerated manner and resorting to criminal law, Goldsmith made himself conspicuous and attracted a great deal of animosity. He was thereby deprived of his coveted reward in the life peerage which he saw as the key to his entry into politics. True, he gained a knighthood. But this was of no political advantage to him and, like all the others on the list, he found himself the object of ridicule. When he changed tack and tried to buy up newspapers, he discovered again that the continuing *Eye* litigation was a major obstacle. How far the case has permanently damaged Goldsmith's career as a would-be press lord, though, remains to be seen. Recent events seem to show that, when times are really hard, journalists are none too fussy about whom they look to for help.

At the same time, far from being smashed, *Private Eye* in many ways thrived as a result of the Goldsmith case. Initially we lost ten thousand or so copies from our circulation, when many of the distributors agreed not to handle the magazine; and in the end we had to pay about £30,000 out of our profits in addition to the £40,000 raised by the Goldenballs Fund. (We must continue, too, to pay the annual contribution of £3,000 towards Goldsmith's costs until the full sum agreed is met.) But it is likely that the extraordinary amount of publicity generated by the case more than helped to restore the circulation that we lost, and in the end the *Eye* emerged as a stronger force, aware that in an emergency it could rely on support from all sorts of unexpected quarters.

The law, meanwhile, remains unchanged, and the case showed vividly how a man with determination and unlimited amounts of money can use it in a number of unprecedented ways. But, in the end, the story goes to confirm the truth of Dr Johnson's saying which I quoted as my text — 'Few attacks either of ridicule or invective make much noise, but by the help of those that they provoke.'

OTHER BOOKS PUBLISHED BY

HARRIMAN HOUSE

'The Official
Lawyer's Handbook'

Can you spot the lawyer?

'One of the most irreverent, funny, and perceptive books about the legal profession has just been published.'*The Times*

'The *Spitting Image* of the legal world: irreverent, biting, and often in delightfully questionable taste.'*The Lawyer*

' .... combines a litany of barbed quips with sound advice.'*The Law Society Gazette*

'A jokey guide to the sleazy world of the solicitor, full of sage advice.'*The Independent on Sunday*

Including advice on the following critical areas :

- **Twnety Good Reasons to become a Lawyer**
  Why not? Everyone else is.
- **Law Society Final**
  Thousands of morons have passed. So can you!
- **Are you Cut out for the Legal Profession?**
  A self-assessment quiz to help you decide — before
  your firm decides for you.

- **Drafting Documents**
  More is better . . . until it begins to make sense.
- **The Art of Billing**
  Who says there are only 24 hours in a day ?
- **Partnership**
  You can make it, if you know what to kiss
  . . . . and whose.
- **Legal Ethics (and other great oxymorons)**
- **How to End a Legal Career**
  Tell a client how the time he's been billed for was
  really spent.

- **Find out what Lawyers Do**
  and how to stop them from doing it to you.
- **How to Handle Romantic Feelings towards a Lawyer**
  Beware the erotic power of Latin.

Over 150,000 copies sold worldwide
Paperback, 220 pages, 40 cartoons, £8.99 ISBN 1 897597 00 2

'The Official
High-Flier's Handbook'

'Very, very funny . . . .' *Business Life Magazine*

'Successfully combines a brisk humour with a huge variety of practical tips' *Business Age Magazine*

"I'm done with sex, and Lord knows I've made enough money, but power — that's something you never get tired of."

Over 250,000 copies sold in the USA.

200 pages including 5 hilarious case studies and 30 cartoons by Pugh. Paperback, ISBN 1 897597 01 0

£7.99 Order form on back page.

CHECK YOUR BUSINESS IQ
• How did you earn your first £10?
Getting straight 'A's in O-levels
Cutting grass and shoveling snow
Starting a chain-letter scheme
Selling grass and cutting snow

GET A HANDLE ON THE BASIC BUSINESS DISCIPLINES
• **Finance** — The study of £££ + how it defies the laws of maths
• **Accounting** — what *really* goes on between the Balance Sheets
• **Marketing** — *push* and *pull*, the dark forces that make 6 year-olds deliver non-negotiable demands for Pop Tarts instead of Alpen
• **Behavioural Theory** — "You've got people skills. You fire him"
• **Production** — what on earth goes on inside the box ?

INPUT: Steel, glass, paint, labour, energy

FACTORY

OUTPUT: Cars

THE FORMULA FOR SUCCESS

$$A \left[\left(\frac{C \times N}{E} \right)^2 + P(B)^3 + G + W \right]^L$$

A = Ambition
B = Buzzword Proficiency
C = CV Expansion
E = Excessive Education
G = Golf Handicap
L = Luck
N = Nerve
P = Power Accessories
W = Work

WOMEN IN BUSINESS
• 8-week Assertiveness Programme to stop your career becoming a remake of *'Bambi Meets Godzilla'*
• Detering the Office Lech : "I'm sorry. The secretarial pool only gave you a '4'."

KEEPING SCORE
• "I founded my own million-pound company, but my sister's a director of ICI. Who's ahead?"
• Signs that your career's on the slide: your office has no desk, no window, and the seat flushes

OFFICE POLITICS & ETIQUETTE
• **Promotion**: You can make it if you know what to kiss . . . and *whose*
• **Work**: remember, the only person who had everything done by Friday was Robinson Crusoe
• **Looks**: why it's gauche to look like an Aztec Sun God in November
• **Sport**: giving the boss 'a customer's game' of squash
• **Sex**: don't get your meat the same place you get your bread
• **Drink**: when to order a Perrier, when to order a Samoan War God
• **First Impressions**: a repertoire of handshakes for every occasion
• Peppering your conversation with the right 'action' words

The Life & Death of
ROCHESTER SNEATH

HUMPHRY BERKELEY

'A delight' — *Times Educational Supplement*

'The funniest book I have read for ages' — *The Daily Telegraph*

'I just laughed and laughed' — *The Times*

'One of our finest humourists' — *Spectator*

'Very, very funny' — *Sunday Times*

'The book that gave me the greatest pleasure' — *Sunday Telegraph*

'A comic masterpiece . . . a laugh on every page' — *New Statesman*

'A cause of hilarity' — *Country Life*

The Times Magazine, July 31st 1993

THE 100 BEST SUMMER BOOKS

'Humphry Berkeley created this appalling character while at Cambridge in 1948. Rochester Sneath was supposedly the headmaster of 'Selhurst', a public school near Petworth, and wrote a series of Henry Root-style letters to genuine headmasters and assorted public figures. He asked the Master of Marlborough how he had 'engineered' a Royal visit, offered advice to the headmaster of Rugby to overlook youthful homosexuality, and invited George Bernard Shaw to address Selhurst on the text 'A Clarion Call to Youth'.

The book is as funny for Sneath's absurd minor-league snobbery as for the replies of his victims. Most were stiffly courteous, but Berkeley carefully remained *just* plausible, and few spotted the scam. This charmingly irresponsible little correspondence is out of print unfortunately. Try your library.'

Hardback, 96 pages, £6.99 ISBN 1 897597 04 5

ORDER FORM

Name: Mr/Mrs/Ms _____

Address: _____

          _____

          _____

Post Code _____

Phone No: _____

Please send me :

☐ x 'The Official *Lawyer*'s Handbook' @ £8.99* = [   ]

☐ x 'The Official *High-Flier*'s Handbook' @ £7.99* = [   ]

☐ x 'The Life & Death of Rochester Sneath' @ £6.99*= [   ]

☐ x 'Goldenballs' @ £9.99* = [   ]

I enclose a cheque payable to 'Harriman House' for £[   ]

Signed . . . . Date . . . .

*All prices include post and packing. At the time of writing, there is no VAT on books. If, when you send in the form, this situation has changed, please add VAT.

 HARRIMAN HOUSE PUBLISHING, 9 IRENE ROAD, PARSONS GREEN, LONDON SW6 4AL